PRAISE FOR THE BEST SELLER

A poignant and powerful gift of story-telling, chock-full of invaluable life lessons, reflective revelations and successful strategies you can implement immediately for a more fulfilling life and for a more profitable business. Not only a relatable and enjoyable reading experience, but an educational and potentially transformational must-read!

— AIMEE COHEN, AUTHOR OF *WOMAN UP!*

An easy and enjoyable read that gives you great guidance to start your sales career. Especially important for those who are used to being successful by sheer force of will and are working in environments that don't give them the tools to grow.

— TONY CAÑAS, CO-FOUNDER OF INSURANCE NERDS AND BEST SELLING AUTHOR OF *INSURING TOMORROW*

The lessons and skills presented are tangible enough that even if you don't currently working in a sales environment, they are applicable to overall personal success.

— CAMMIE LATTA, DIRECTOR OF MARKETING

The unwritten rules behind why winners win.

— KEN LUALLEN, BUSINESS DEVELOPMENT

The Best Seller reads like a novel which allows you to relate to the characters in a real life manner. I love and appreciate how the main character experiences failure and struggles while trying to complete the steps and rules explained in the book. It reminds us that building relationships and gaining trust takes work but the end result is so worth it.

— GENA DIMURO, SALES COORDINATOR

I highly recommend this read! Even if you're not in business sales as a career, like me, you will still learn a tremendous amount about how to improve your relationships, interactions and to leverage your chances for life going more your way, with the bonus of helping other people. The book embodies living with a win-win mindset in any relationship.

— KELLY JENSEN, CO-COORDINATOR OF LOCAL MOPS CHAPTER AND EDUCATOR

THE BEST SELLER

A Novel About Access, Relationships, and Harnessing the Power of a Paceline to Propel You Forward in Life and in Business.

KATIE R. BISHOP
DOUG REICHARDT

Camerado Publishing

Copyrighted Material

The Best Seller

Copyright © 2020 by Camerado, LLC
All Rights Reserved.

No part of this publication may be reproduced, stored in a retrieval system or transmitted, in any form or by any means – electronic, mechanical, photocopying, recording or otherwise – without prior written permission from the publisher, except for the inclusion of brief quotations in a review.

For information about this title or to order other books and/or electronic media, contact the publisher:

Camerado, LLC
legalnotices@camerado.net

Copyright acknowledgements appear in the References section of this book.

ISBNs:
Paperback: 978-1-7341505-0-6
Hardcover: 978-1-7341505-1-3
eBook: 978-1-7341505-2-0
Library of Congress Control Number: 2020900493

Printed in the United States of America

CONTENTS

Introduction — ix
Author's Note — xi

PART ONE

1. The Light of Day — 3
2. Street Magician — 5
3. Gravity's Pull — 9
4. The Hand & The Voice — 14
5. Parasitic Drag — 21
6. The Pain Of Change — 26
7. A Look Back — 31
8. First Impressions — 35
9. Clean Slate — 40
10. I-Caps — 48
11. Vision — 52

PART TWO

12. The First Lesson — 57
13. Tree Branch — 65
14. Positioning — 70
15. Bounces and Deposits — 80
16. Start Where You Are — 90
17. A Systematic Approach — 93
18. Deposit First — 95
19. Next Step — 100
20. Extra Mile — 104
21. Hitting Send — 106
22. Shifting Perspective — 110
23. Preparation Matters — 117
24. Logic And Intuition — 124
25. Customer Centered — 130
26. Game Plan Preparation — 136
27. Living With Humility — 140

28. Communicate Effectively   145

PART THREE
29. Behind The Scenes   151
30. Craft Your Message   155
31. Own Your Direction   161
32. Creating Alignment   166
33. Measuring Cost   172
34. Digging Deeper   175
35. Always Learning, Always Growing   177
36. Gaining a Different Perspective   182
37. Communicating Value   186

PART FOUR
38. Timing   193
39. Podium Stand   195
40. Breakaway   199
41. Aerodynamics   206
42. Road Rash   214
43. Cross Training   216
44. The Drivetrain   219
45. Cat 5 Tattoo   223
46. Team Time Trial   226
47. Paceline   230
48. The Sprint   234
49. Focus   239

PART FIVE
50. Landing A Client   245
51. The Next Level   250
52. Getting Positioned   252
53. A Different Line   257
54. Developing Trust   262
55. Clipped   268
56. Leading a Life of Significance   272
57. Changing Course   278
58. The Best Seller   285

Acknowledgments	291
References	293

*Dedicated to Debbie Reichardt,
the great influence behind both authors.
Thank you for your fierce love, guidance, and wisdom.*

INTRODUCTION

The Best Seller is not your typical business book and that is on purpose. The narrative that unfolds is a snippet of life, bringing in true stories from the past and fictional characters of the present to illustrate a greater perspective. The Best Seller coaches on how to be mentored and sponsored, how to mentor and sponsor others, and why it matters. More importantly, The Best Seller unveils the behind-the-scenes secrets of favorable access and demand-pull to help others become The Best Seller in their businesses.

Doug Reichardt built the sales content of this book from his successful career in sales and leadership. His work as a one-on-one mentor has helped hundreds of young professionals win in the sales world. You won't find Doug on social media but you will find him in coffee shops where he mentors business people around the globe.

Doug's daughter, Katie Bishop, wrote the stories in this book, not as The Best Seller, but as the curious student looking to improve her own sales ability. Her passion is to help the next generation avoid the pitfalls that so many of us make early in our careers.

INTRODUCTION

Neither Doug nor Katie could have written this book without the other. They used their individual strengths and relied on each other to fill in the gaps through their personal experiences and skills. Together, they created a paceline.

A paceline is a formation in which people create a draft for others to follow. Throughout the process, key players rotate to the front and everyone contributes. The formation of the paceline increases the effectiveness of each individual in the group and the group as a whole. People moving together with paceline power achieve more than those traveling solo. There is no draft riding solo. You cannot learn to be The Best Seller without the power of a paceline.

As you'll learn, becoming The Best Seller takes time. Time is precious and you get to choose how you spend your moments. There are two main ways to read this book:

Option 1: You want to read this with the utmost efficiency and learn about the business content only. Please skip to Part Two without any guilt and read through Part Three. The end. If you like what you read, then go back and read the other Parts. Tell us what you think @ www.KatieBishop.us

Option 2: You want to relate to the content, read something meaningful, and learn the trusted techniques to help you become The Best Seller. Please start with Part One and read through to the end. Test out the Steps & Rules in your work and personal life. Refer back often and tell us what you think @ www.KatieBishop.us

Connect with us: www.KatieBishop.us

IG: @KatieBishop.us
#pacelinepower #thebestsellersalesbook
#demandpull #favorableaccess

Facebook: facebook.com/KatieBishop.us

AUTHOR'S NOTE

The idea of this book was born when Katie joined fifteen other college students on a 220 mile canoe journey down the Connecticut River from Hanover, New Hampshire to the Long Island Sound. During the adventure, she talked with fellow students about family. Katie shared that she wanted to capture the lessons and stories of her grandfather, Bill Reichardt, with live interviews and experiences working alongside him in his mentoring. She discarded that idea after graduation because she wanted to chart her own course for the future and not look to the past.

Perspective is a game-changer. Katie's early failed work experiences taught her that when we learn from history we can improve the future. Years later, when she became a parent, she began to understand the depth and breadth of work required when raising the next generation. She started to fully appreciate the work and wisdom of those who had traveled the roads before her.

While Katie and her husband parented their young kids and

worked in Colorado, acquaintances from Iowa asked her what they could give to her father, Doug, to thank him for mentoring them. Curious, she asked her dad about this mentoring. He answered that a few of his mentees told him he needed to write a book. Doug was not going to write a book on his own so he asked the mentees to capture the Steps & Rules that he had taught to hundreds of young business professionals over the decades. The original list that they compiled had eleven Steps and twenty-six Rules. They then advised Doug that he needed to find a writer.

For five years, Doug and Katie wrestled with storylines, condensed Steps & Rules, and created a paceline that pushed and pulled them along this writing journey. In the process, Doug's Best Seller strategies helped to make Katie a better seller in her sales career. With time and practice, she knows that she can become The Best Seller and so can you.

In early reviews, Doug and Katie were asked which stories and characters were real and which were the result of the creative process in The Best Seller. Lives before the year 2000 were not as well documented as they are today, but archived newspapers, books, photos, videos, and stories allowed for Bill's life, detailed in Chapter 6 through Chapter 32, to be depicted as accurately as possible. Beyond that, the stories and characters have been based on genuine experiences, but the creative process paved the way.

PART ONE

History

THE LIGHT OF DAY

Chapter 1

As the elevator doors opened to her apartment lobby, Mackenzie was startled by a man's booming voice. Trying to keep her metal bike cleats from clacking on the tile floor, she waddled on her heels to catch a glimpse of whoever could be so oblivious to the unwritten code of quiet in the early morning. He sounded old. Perhaps he was hard of hearing.

She craned her neck around the corner to find the lobby's television blaring a commercial showcasing business suits. The old man's voice thundered, "Because they're quality. And there just isn't any substitute for quality…" The voice and lines were familiar, but she was so miffed at the noise that she didn't care who was talking, she just wanted to turn it off.

Just as she was about to press the 'power' button, the video panned to a familiar face. She stopped to stare. She hadn't seen his commercial in years. He looked much older, but he was immaculately dressed, as usual. His voice continued, "No sale is ever final here. We have courteous and competent personnel here. We guarantee your complete satisfaction when you shop here." Her initial annoyance disappeared as his reassuring presence and words soothed her. She smiled as she recited the end of his commercial with him, "And I'll see to it. Because I'm here. I'm Bill Reichardt, and I own the store."

Mackenzie warmly remembered how she and her mom had recited those final lines to each other so much that it became an inside joke. It wasn't a funny or flashy commercial. Neither of them had ever met Bill Reichardt, but through that commercial, they felt like they knew him and felt like they could trust him. He seemed like a person who stood by his word, someone who cared, someone who set a course in life and followed through. Or, maybe they liked that commercial just because they liked knowing that someone was where he said he would be.

Over the years, Mackenzie's mom had been creative in her attempts to give excuses for why her dad never showed up when he promised to be there. It had happened so often that she wasn't surprised when he didn't even stop by before she left for college. Her mom, sensing his pending absence, had wheeled out an unexpected gift. "I found this for you at a garage sale, but the owner said that it's made with quality parts. And, you know, there just isn't any substitute for quality…" Despite their underlying sadness with her dad's absence, they both laughed at her mom's attempt to imitate the TV businessman who felt like a wise grandfather figure to both of them.

Mackenzie walked towards the apartment complex bike rack to unlock the chains holding her wearied Schwinn road bike. The Schwinn had been her constant companion in the past six years, taking her through the hills and valleys of college and the following two years of wandering from job to job. In the past few months, her bike hadn't seen the light of day. Neither had she.

STREET MAGICIAN
Chapter 2

Last night, she wanted to ridicule her friend's idea. She wanted to let Luke know that he didn't have a clue as to what she wanted or needed and she certainly did not need his pity. *He is so arrogant to think that he could fix my work problems by suggesting I join a cycling group,* she thought. *Luke doesn't know the first thing about sales, let alone networking. He's a computer programmer who sits in a cubicle all day long, for crying out loud.*

But, he had used some business terms that she hadn't heard, even in all of her marketing classes in college. Using the new terms, he made the impression that he knew more than she expected. She couldn't remember exactly how he worded the terms, but one was described as 'favorable' and another one was some hyphenated use of 'demand.' She was curious as to how those words could be relevant to a cycling group and to business. What Luke said had piqued her interest, but the main driver for her agreeing to join him was that deep down she knew she needed to change her current route. The status quo was definitely not working.

Mackenzie clicked into her shiny upgraded pedals and coasted on the empty road before her. She shifted her grip and remembered her spin instructor's advice from three months prior, "Your position on the bike and your connection to the bike matters. First, adjust your seat and handlebars to maximize your leverage. Second, what you wear and how it fits, matters. Running shoes and toe cages don't give you a solid bond with your bike. Your foot shifts around as you push your pedals and you lose power as you climb hills. Rather than wasting your energy, you need to wear a cleated shoe to connect with the pedal system. This connects you to the bike, allowing you to build a steady rhythm as you pedal the full circle."

Mackenzie had stayed after class one night to ask her favorite spin instructor, Lisa, to teach her more about how to pedal the 'full circle.' Lisa, whose calves were sculpted with thousands of cycling miles and whose practical pixie hairstyle, peppered with flecks of gray, matched her military intensity, ordered her to hop back on the spin bike. As she rotated Mackenzie's foot around the pedaling circle, she began to explain, "Most beginner cyclists use only one section of the pedal rotation – they push on the down stroke. While that is the most powerful part of your stroke, cleated shoes and pedals allow all of the leg muscles to work more effectively by letting you pull up and set up the other leg for maximum efficiency." Lisa paused and looked at Mackenzie. Mackenzie was leaning forward in concentration, taking in every word.

Lisa continued, "With a cleated system, your foot is in constant connection to the pedal, which is connected to the crank, which is connected to the drivetrain of the bike. You and the cycling system work together as one. Your connection gives you direct access to the leveraging power of the system."

The next spin class started to trickle in at that point, so Lisa wrapped up her talk, "Mackenzie, it's hard work changing the way you've always done things. Most people struggle when they learn a new method because continuing with old habits is easier than training yourself to learn new habits. Most bikers under stress revert back to the clunky push pedal stroke because it's what they are used to. You have to constantly practice this advanced technique to train your other muscles before it becomes a new habit and before you'll experience the full benefits. You'll be a stronger biker all around, and your knee will recover quicker when you intentionally increase its range of motion; the full circle rotation uses all of the major muscles connected to the knee. So stick with it."

Lisa began to walk away, but then changed her mind and added, "When you want to get outside of this cycling lab and apply these lessons on the road outdoors, let me know. I can teach you a few more techniques for maximizing your potential in a paceline."

As Mackenzie walked out of the spin room that night, she whipped out her phone to purchase pedals for her Schwinn road bike that would pair with her cleated spin shoes. Lisa's talk had hit a nerve. Mackenzie desperately wanted to maximize her potential in anything. Her knee injury hadn't just minimized her college track career; it had ended it. With one bad step, her goals and aspirations snapped like her ACL. As her identity of 'athlete' shriveled away, like her atrophied quad post-surgery, her confidence crumbled and her future plans dissolved.

She had taken an entry level job after college, followed by another, as she tried to figure out what to do with her life. She listened to podcasts and scrolled social media posts that told her to follow her passion, but nothing ignited her to figure out how to start that journey.

Instead, she numbly scanned online job postings and randomly applied to the ones that sounded somewhat interesting. Anything seemed more interesting than the data entry boredom she was dealing with day in and day out.

She had forced her way through one particular interviewer's questions, projecting an image of who she wanted to be, "As a college athlete who pushed through the physical pain of rehabilitating my knee after surgery, I'm well-trained to tackle tough situations with perseverance."

She was shocked to receive the job offer with zero experience. Relieved that she would have a job that could finally cover all of her bills, she allowed herself to think that if she could land a sales job when she was totally unqualified, then surely she could jump into sales, work hard, and succeed. *How hard could selling be? Call some people and sell something. Done and done.*

In the past three months, though, she hadn't even gotten close to landing any sales, which meant no commissions for her. Her sales teams' weekly meetings had begun to create knots in her stomach as she tried to mask her failure behind her fabricated list of potential clients. Even if all she heard was the voicemail of a sales suspect, she listed that sales suspect in the Sales Excellence System, or SES, as a prospect. According to her sales manager, Stan, the metrics in the SES could predict who would succeed and who would fail to hit their sales forecast.

She did not want to be more of a failure than she already felt. So she continuously shuffled her list around like a street magician hiding a ball under one of three cups. She was not good at shuffling; her awkwardness was obvious to her and everyone else around the sales table. Each week, her anxiety escalated, and she withdrew more frequently into her apartment where she could hide from her incompetence at work. She hadn't been on a spin bike in two months, and her newly installed pedals on her road bike had remained shiny and unused.

Taking a deep breath on the empty road ahead of her, she nodded to herself with approval. Accepting Luke's invitation to this morning's cycling ride was a good idea. She felt the cold claws of anxiety from work thaw with the warmth of activity. She whispered to the wind, "Today is a new day."

GRAVITY'S PULL
Chapter 3

She had thrown on her windbreaker jacket knowing that it would keep out the chill of the morning breeze, wouldn't weigh her down, and would conveniently mask her late night carb intake during the past few months. But the noise of the windbreaker flapping against itself was beginning to irritate her. She second-guessed her choice of gear as she approached the cycling group's meet-up spot.

Feeling nervous about her first group cycling ride, she was relieved to hear the familiar 'bing' of a text message from her phone in her bike seat bag and mused, *I bet that's Luke letting me know he's at the coffee shop. I think I was too harsh to him last night because I just feel so stuck at work. He's really changed since college, in a good way. He's not so focused on himself anymore.*

The "Dynamo Coffee Shop" appeared across the street. She lightly applied her brakes until her bike slowed and she focused on unclipping from her pedals. The cleats didn't slide out as easily on her road bike as she remembered them sliding out on the spin bike, but she was able to twist her right foot hard enough to hear the snap of metal which allowed her to place her foot on the cement.

She retrieved her phone to see the text from Luke, "Have to go in early for work. Big opportunity for me. Can't make it to ride."

A familiar and painful twinge of abandonment surged through her. She texted back, upset that he ditched her at an early morning ride where she now, would know no one. "Seriously? I'm at the coffee shop already. Can't believe you bailed on me last minute."

She stared at her phone, waiting for his reply, silently pleading Luke to change his mind and drive over. Nothing. The time read 5:45 AM. She steeled herself and muttered, "Ugh. Maybe he hasn't changed. No thought to anyone but himself. Whatever. I'm here. Let's do this."

She fiercely snapped back into her pedals to ride across the street to Dynamo Coffee. As she neared the entrance, she again applied the brakes and started to unclip from her pedals. Her bike stopped, but neither bike shoe would unclip. She gave one more frantic jerk of her right shoe before succumbing to gravity's pull.

With no escape from the impending slow motion crash, she thought, *what a perfect analogy to my current work situation: trapped and looking like a fool while everyone watches me fall.*

She landed hard on the curb. Pain coursed through her hand and hip as she slammed into the cement. She cursed her pedals and muttered angrily, "That's it! I don't belong here. What was I thinking?" She focused on her left foot, not wanting to look around and confirm her fears that everyone saw her fail to complete the most basic move of dismounting a bicycle. She shook her head. If Luke had been with her, they could have laughed together at the ridiculousness of the situation. But, he wasn't. *That is the last time I take Luke's advice on anything.*

She twisted her left foot again as she heard a rugged voice ask, "Are you okay?"

Mackenzie could feel the heat rising on her face as she

turned her head towards the voice. Her eyes stopped at the chiseled, golden tan legs in front of her. Too stunned to respond, she questioned herself, *am I imagining things? Did I hit my head?*

"May I lend you a hand?" he offered. She looked at his face and was dumbstruck. She extended her hand to his and he lifted her and her bicycle up from the curb.

She forgot about Luke. She freed her left foot from its captor. He stepped back. Mesmerized by his eyes, blue like the sky after a storm, she stepped toward him with her free foot. Her right foot, still entrapped in the other pedal, tripped her then hurled her into the bicycle handlebars. Mackenzie and her bike catapulted into the strong arms of her rescuer in shiny black spandex.

"Whoa, there girl! Got you." He chuckled as he gently made sure she wouldn't fall over again. Although she felt like a clumsy fool, she smiled genuinely at her good luck.

He grinned while holding her bike steady, "Unclip from that pedal, shake yourself off, and I'll introduce you to a few people. My name's Wes."

Mackenzie high-fived herself mentally and admired her rescuer, "Wes," she repeated, dreamily, then realized she needed to snap herself out of her daze. "I'm Mackenzie. I can't thank you enough for your help."

"That's nothing. Cleats can be tricky little buggers, just takes some practice getting used to 'em. Last week, we rolled up to a stop sign, and the guy next to me was having trouble clipping out. He fell away from me, taking four other guys down like dominos! You landed rather gracefully on that curb. Bonus points for not pushing anyone else down while you were falling."

Mackenzie gave a relaxed smile. Wes scanned the parking lot and asked, "So what brings you out to the ride this mornin'?"

Before Mackenzie could answer, Wes interrupted the brief silence, "There she is. Jules! Come on over here!"

As Jules walked over, Mackenzie's heart lurched. Mackenzie could tell, even from a distance, that this diva had put serious effort into looking her best that morning. The light from the coffee shop highlighted a purple hue in her jet-black curled waves. Her expertly manicured eyebrows formed a sly scowl as she looked down her pale, pointed nose at Mackenzie.

Wes swooned at Jules. Jules batted her false eyelashes at him and caressed his arm. When they turned back towards Mackenzie, Mackenzie noticed that her long eyelashes did nothing to hide the cold stare in her gray eyes. Wes broke the ice, "Mackenzie, this is my girlfriend, Jules. We've been training for our first cycling race coming up next month. Jules, this is Mackenzie. Mackenzie, this is your first time joinin' this cycling group, right?"

Mackenzie's reverie grinded to a halt. "Hi Jules, it's nice to meet you. Yes, this is my first ride. My friend, *Luke*, invited me…" Mackenzie emphasized Luke's name to try to warm up her cold glare.

Luke's name dropped unnoticed by Jules. Mackenzie's enthusiasm waned as she strained to keep her voice upbeat. Jules moved closer to Wes, making sure to signal her stake in him. Jules did remind Mackenzie of some kind of jewel, something that was beautiful with sharp edges.

Maybe I'm too quick to judge, she pondered, *but why is it that women are so untrusting of other women?* Sure, a few moments ago, she imagined riding off into the sunrise with Wes to begin their happily-ever-after story. But, once he mentioned the word girlfriend, Mackenzie just wanted him to take Jules towards the sun and stay with her until she melted.

Mackenzie grasped for her exit and forced her best smile, "Your boyfriend was nice enough to dust off my wounded pride after I tipped over like a lame cow. Haha. I'm going to grab an iced coffee and apply it to my bruised ego. It's so nice meeting you. Best of luck to you both on your upcoming race!"

Mackenzie waved good-bye too eagerly as she walked her bike to the front of the coffee shop. She internally kicked herself. *Lame cow? That's the best I could come up with? So much for things looking up. I bet Jules will have all the other women turn against me before this ride is over. This day is quickly spiraling down into some dark vortex, and it's not even 6 AM yet. I'd better grab some serious caffeine.*

THE HAND & THE VOICE

Chapter 4

As she stood in the coffee line, she examined the brightly dressed cyclists gathered together in small clusters. Warm greetings and slaps on the back were exchanged. Laughter erupted from a group of fit fifty year old men taking shots of espresso like twenty-two year-olds with tequila. She wanted whatever they were having and opted for the espresso shot, hoping it would give her the lift she needed to survive the morning.

At 5:58 AM, headlight beams filled the parking lot like a cloud of fireflies. More cyclists poured out of their cars, unloaded their bikes and coasted to the coffee shop entrance. Mackenzie spotted a few women gathered together and started to make her way over to them, hoping that the more mature women would be more welcoming than Jules. Before she could introduce herself, someone whistled sharply, which silenced the mingling.

A slender and muscled man in his sixties began to talk, "Happy Tuesday, everyone. Looks like we have a great group today. Cycling Group A is for those who want to ride at a near threshold. Group B is the endurance group. If you're new today,

I suggest starting in Group B. Know that we will not leave anyone behind on the road. We're glad to have you.

"Today's route: we'll ride through Water Works Park and have a sprint coming off the top of the water tower. Then find your rhythm and ride down the Great Western Trail and loop back via Veterans Parkway and Park Avenue. We'll double that loop. Group A, you'll take that four times. Let's have a great ride."

At his closing word, everyone hopped on their bikes and started rolling out. Mackenzie scrambled over to what she thought was Group B, trying to position herself close to the group of middle aged women and away from Jules.

The route was uphill right out of the gate, but it seemed fairly easy, so Mackenzie believed she could keep up. After all, it had only been two months since her last spin class.

They navigated down the side streets and shot out into Water Works Park, the expansive greenbelt just west of downtown. The black-topped bike trail was canopied by enormous oak trees lining the path. All Mackenzie could hear was the whiz of the wheels and the crisp morning breeze whipping across her ears, with the occasional flap from her windbreaker.

Mackenzie saw the big water tower up ahead and tried to take in a few deep breaths knowing that they were about to have their first sprint. She started to feel winded but hoped everyone else did too. A woman's voice beside her asked, "How ya holding up?"

"Doing okay," Mackenzie admitted.

Mackenzie glanced at the woman to give her a half smile, and the woman responded, "Well, that was the warm-up. So make sure to stay close and catch a draft."

Mackenzie's face tightened. The group started picking up speed as they neared the water tower. She forgot about technique and started pushing as hard as she could to keep up on the sprint.

Once on the Great Western Trail, they hit a series of rollers. Slight uphill, slight downhill, as the pace picked up steadily. Mackenzie started struggling to stay close to the pack. Three riders shot past her making her feel like she was rolling backwards. The throbbing in her hand and hip resurfaced, her knee surgery scars pulsed, and her lungs burned. Mackenzie thought, *I'm not going to make it. I should cut my losses now and no one will notice.*

Suddenly, just as Mackenzie started to let up, she felt a supportive hand on her mid-back which accelerated her like an electric motor. She looked to her left as a man's voice said, "Keep your eyes looking ahead. Downshift, take the pressure off your legs and just spin. I got ya." The Hand felt like a lifeline, guiding her back from the edge of quitting.

Mackenzie downshifted gears and spun her legs, loosening up her leg muscles. The gap between her and the main pack narrowed as she caught her breath. She started to pedal again, but The Voice told her, "Don't put any pressure on the pedals. Recover. I'll let you know when to pedal."

Feeling grateful for the help, but flustered that someone sensed she needed it, she looked straight ahead and did what The Voice told her. After another minute passed, she had regained some strength. Once they reconnected with the main pack, The Hand gave her a gentle push and let go. She didn't get a chance to thank The Voice connected to The Hand.

The pack stayed together until the next big descent. She looked at the bike speedometer next to her and saw the speeds climbing: 20mph...24mph...28mph. She felt like she was flying. Feeling good about herself, she was caught off-guard when she heard shouts, "On your left! Group A on your left!"

As the speeding paceline powered by, she looked at the flashy bikes and slick gear they wore. Her pack started to speed up with the passing group. Shocked and frustrated that her speed wasn't fast enough to keep up, she dropped further and further off of the group. She shifted her gears to compensate for the gap, stood up on her bike and pushed with all she had on the down stroke, too tired to pull up on the upstroke. Although she was pushing harder, she was falling back farther. *What am I doing wrong? Why can't I keep up? What had Lisa tried to share about the full circle?* Even though she knew it was important, she simply did not have the capacity to dredge up that advice.

The Hand landed on her back again, like an old friend.

"Thank you," she panted for breath.

The Voice returned, "Relax. Spin with me. We'll bridge the gap."

The Hand continued to push her along as The Voice continued, "Cycling seems like an easy sport, but you can't expect to jump on a bike and ride well; it's best to learn from those who have traveled the road before you. When you're first getting started, you need to position yourself in the paceline to observe the group dynamics. To do this, you first have to figure out which riders you can follow; then, align yourself with the wheel in front of you and mimic the motion. Today, do not go to the front of the group…unless you are trying to prove something…"

Magically, with steady ease, they closed the gap again, and she felt propelled by The Hand. She jockeyed into the middle of the paceline. Nervous about being so close to all of the riders in the paceline, she briefly considered dropping back. But she realized it was an easier ride there in the middle than it was from the back.

She had read a few cycling articles about the draft, but it wasn't until she was mimicking the motions of those ahead of her and feeling the pull of the draft, that she could truly understand the difference the draft made. The shorter the distance between her and the support rider in front of her, the more favorable the head wind resistance and the greater the efficiency. *So this is how cyclists riding in a paceline draft save up to forty percent in energy over cyclists riding solo.*

One by one, the lead rider dropped back and the next rider took the lead. As they rotated through, Mackenzie moved closer to the front. She felt strong and began her move up. Inexplicably, she found herself at the front of the group. Wanting to redeem herself from needing a rescue, she pushed her pedals as hard as she could and willed herself to stay there longer than the last person. Her heart pumped wildly until she couldn't go any faster. She peeled off the front, totally wiped out. Her wheels slowed so quickly that she couldn't even catch the last rider of the group.

Her head slumped down, she gasped for breath, and attempted to drag her cement-block-legs while her heart pounded out of her chest. The Voice whispered from behind her, "What was that all about?"

His question quickly reminded her that she had failed to heed The Voice's earlier advice. *Why didn't I follow what he said to do? Why did I have to do it my way?*

She didn't have the oxygen to respond and focused instead on trying to breathe. The Voice continued as The Hand returned to her back, "Align yourself with the wheel in front of you and mimic the motion. And do *not* go to the front...unless you are trying to prove something."

"I was. In rotation. I had to," she pleaded, gasping for breath.

The Voice responded, "Nope. You didn't. You weren't ready to go to the front," The Voice was stern but gentle. "How are you feeling?"

"Wiped. Out," she labored. Then, with The Hand pushing her forward as she downshifted to take the resistance off, between breaths she asked, "Why. Are you. Back here?"

"This is a no-drop ride. Today, I'm what we call, 'The Sweeper.' That means I'm here so that no one gets left behind. I'm here to make sure you don't drop off or out."

She managed, "I'm ready. To do. Both."

"Well, you do have a choice here in a few minutes. We're on

the backside of the loop. The main group is going to take one more loop before heading back. There will be a few riders peeling off early. You can peel off with them, or you can take the next loop. Your choice."

Mackenzie's heart rate had recovered slightly, and she was finally able to breathe more slowly, "Is it ok if I peel off? Not sure you can push me for another loop," she gave him a sideways grin.

The Voice chuckled. "I like your spunk. You remind me of my daughter. Great athlete, stubborn as all get-out, but can always laugh at herself. You should head back early. And you should come back and ride with us again on Thursday. You have the potential to be a very strong biker. You have good strength in your legs. Not so much in your ears, though," he laughed as he took The Hand away. "Next time, I want you to think about and practice what I told you. Can you do that?"

Mackenzie nodded, "Yes, absolutely. I will. Thank you. I'm sorry I didn't listen. I think I just wanted to prove that I could hold my own."

"In time, you can do that. But you need to learn from those around you first," The Voice remarked.

Clearly, I have a lot to learn, she said to herself. "I really appreciate your help. I'm Mackenzie. I'm sorry; I didn't catch your name?" she asked.

"JD," The Voice named himself.

"Thanks, JD," Mackenzie said, in earnest.

"No problem. And two more things before you go," JD applied his brakes to slow down near the turn off. Coasting straight ahead, he sat up and turned to look directly at her, "First, what you wear is important. Find yourself a bike jersey. When you're on a bike, a windbreaker acts like a parachute and makes you work harder while making you much less efficient. Wear a bike jersey to decrease the wind drag. When you next jump out of a plane, you can wear that parachute to slow you down before you hit the ground."

Her cheeks flushed. She hadn't thought that her lightweight windbreaker would slow her down by catching the wind. She laughed at herself and said, "Got it."

"Second. Small adjustments matter. Pump up your tires to the specs. You'll decrease what's called 'rolling resistance.' Wind resistance and rolling resistance create 'parasitic drag.'"

She didn't fully understand what he was saying about parasitic drag, but it sounded like something she should definitely try to avoid. "Will do. Thanks again, JD. See you Thursday." She watched as JD swiftly picked up his pace and pedaled out of sight. She guessed that he had once been a professional cyclist, probably sponsored by Specialized, judging from all the labeling and branding on his gear.

PARASITIC DRAG
Chapter 5

When Mackenzie arrived at the office, she tackled her cold-call list with renewed energy. The cycling ride had jarred the foggy feeling in her brain that recently plagued her at work. Her attitude was buoyant and her voice, lifted with a genuine enthusiasm over the phone, didn't waver after her first dozen dead-end calls.

The cubicles around her buzzed with the efforts of her fellow OnBoardMobile 'sales crew,' as their Sales Manager called them. This sales crew of newly hired twenty-somethings had started out eager to prove their worth and ready to learn from OnBoardMobile's training program and revolutionary mobile application. The company's technology allowed them to review all training techniques at any time during the day with the latest content. The content was provided by the more seasoned sales leaders in the company and did an excellent job educating them on how to close the sale. If she ever got to the point of closing the sale, she would be ready. Unfortunately, the only thing she saw get closed in the past three months were the doors she was trying to open.

At 9 AM, an email arrived in her inbox. As she read it, she

felt the momentum of the day drag to a stop. She guessed that if there was 'parasitic drag' in the workplace, this was it.

From: Stan Sillenger
Date: Tuesday, 9:00 AM
To: Sales Crew
Subject: Activity Standards

Sales Crew,

Now that you've had a few months to learn the best sales pitches from our OnBoardMobile training app, it's time to educate you on the metrics of success. This sales crew will be ramping up to our company standards of Sales Excellence.

Across the country, our seasoned sales team is measured by these Sales Excellence metrics. Going forward, you will record all of your metrics through our Sales Excellence System (SES). When you see that your activity is not lining up with the expected metrics, you will know where to focus for better results.

It is essential that you record every activity, every outgoing phone call attempt, every direct email sent, every meeting, and every conversation. In order to count all sales suspects in the sales process, it is necessary to enter them into and then move them through the system into each subsequent phase. Your employment and compensation will be measured by these activity metrics:

Main weekly activities:

- Cold calls
- Phone call follow-ups
- In-person meetings
- Demonstrations
- Attendance at networking events

Additional activities:

- Brochure mailings
- Social Media messages

We will have follow-up communication regarding how you compare against one another on this sales crew. You will be able to visually see who is most successful and why based on the number of activities each salesperson is creating in our SES system. This is a proven methodology, and the activity metrics tell the story.

To Sales Excellence,
Stan

Mackenzie heard the audible groans from her sales crew indicating that they were reading the email at the same time she was. Mackenzie placed her hand on her forehead to lessen the sudden drain of energy. *How do activity metrics tell the story? I'm making more cold calls than anyone on this sales crew! Competing and being compared against each other is certainly one way to motivate. But isn't there a better way?*

Mackenzie overheard one of her co-workers say, "I'm going to take a whizz, make sure to input that in the Sales Excellence System for me, will ya?" His two cubicle neighbors buckled over with laughter and Mackenzie chuckled silently.

Clearly, Mackenzie wasn't the only one who needed some relief. This added pressure of detailed sales excellence metrics was a drag, to say the least. She didn't see how recording the metrics of her cold calls would get her any closer to making a sale.

There had to be a better process other than just pushing through the gauntlet of cold calls. She needed to know how to bridge the gap between the cold-call list and the close pitch from her OnBoardMobile training.

Bridge the gap. Those words brought her thoughts back to the morning's bike ride. JD's support had helped her to bridge the gap between where she was and where she wanted to go. Right before The Sweeper pushed her back into position, she had already given up on the ride.

Her work and personal life in the past few months felt exactly like the part of the morning where she was ditched by Luke, tipped like a helpless cow in front of strangers, and left in the dust by the cycling group. In the past few months, she felt ditched by the manager who had promised to give her useful training, she constantly made mistakes at work in front of people she barely knew, and she was measured against the company's top salespeople who were so far ahead of her that there was no chance of catching up.

If only there could be a Sweeper in my work life. She sighed, *dream on, Mackenzie*. Stan, her manager, expected every salesperson to make their own way through the cold calls. He directly stated that if any person from the sales crew could not close a total of six-figure sales by the end of the year, he or she would be fired without severance. They had agreed to those stipulations when they signed their contract upon hiring.

Mackenzie remembered signing that document hoping that their OnBoardMobile training was as good as they said it would be. She didn't have another option. It hadn't been more than three weeks into the training when Stan had explicitly told her that she might not have the potential to make it at OnBoardMobile.

JD told her that she had potential.

I may not have potential in sales, but at least I have potential in something, she thought.

She made a decision to persist with the cycling club and wanted to text someone to make it official. "Going back to the group ride on Thursday. You in?" she texted Luke.

He responded, "Can't Thurs, still pushing through work crisis. They need me. Estimating I'll be able to rejoin in a week or two. You had fun?"

"Wouldn't call it fun, but definitely learned a few things," she typed.

"Cool. Looking forward to seeing you soon," he typed back.

Despite her still being upset that he ditched her, his response made her smile.

THE PAIN OF CHANGE
Chapter 6

When Thursday morning rolled around, she shot out of bed, ready to put JD's cycling tips into practice. She rode to the Dynamo shop wearing an old bike jersey that her packrat roommate found for her and was pleased thinking about her obvious reduction in wind resistance. Her tires were pumped to the proper PSI, reducing her rolling resistance. She felt confident knowing she had reduced her overall parasitic drag and her mind was ready to ride. As she neared the shop, she reminded herself, "Align with the wheel in front of you. Do not go to the front of the group, and for goodness sakes, remember to unclip before you stop."

Although Mackenzie arrived early to the ride and scanned the cyclists for JD, she didn't see him. She spotted a group of women riders and worked her way through the crowd, hoping to introduce herself to someone.

The women were engaged in their own conversations. Mackenzie inched closer to overhear a few conversations, hoping that she could latch onto something someone said and ease her way into the group. She brought out her phone and flipped through a few old text messages in order to appear occupied.

She couldn't think of a clever way to enter the conversations, so she stood there, scrolling senselessly.

After the group leader talked through their route, Mackenzie saw a friendly looking woman wearing a bright blue jersey, matching blue, mirrored sunglasses and a blue helmet. Mackenzie took a deep breath before introducing herself, "Hey, I'm new to the cycling group, and you flew by me last time. Would you mind if I tried to keep up with you today?" She felt like she was back at work, cold-calling for an invitation.

The woman in blue responded, "Oh, hi there. I do think I saw you on Tuesday's ride. Well, I'm training for a race next month, so I'll be riding hard today. You may want to ask that group over there," she pointed. "I'm sure they'd be happy to let you join them."

After three months of cold-calling strangers, Mackenzie thought she should be used to the feelings of rejection by now. She wasn't.

"Thanks!" she forced. She pushed herself to walk in the direction of where the woman pointed.

Mackenzie didn't ask permission of anyone in this next group. As they began riding, she just positioned herself in the back, pretending she was supposed to be there. Although she didn't exchange any words with the riders around her, she did focus on putting JD's lessons into practice, which gave her a sense of accomplishment.

At the end of the ride, she spotted JD and ran up to him, re-introducing herself.

JD smiled and said, "Thanks for the reminder of your name. So, how'd you do today, Mackenzie?"

"I did not wear a parachute," Mackenzie gestured to her jersey, "I aligned with the wheel in front of me. I did not go to the front of the group. I rode the entire route. I'd say I did a lot better today. What do you think?"

"Good work," JD affirmed.

"JD, how long have you been cycling?" Mackenzie felt the need to know more about JD and asked the first question that came to her mind.

"I bought my first road bike when I was 46. It took me a few years to understand what this sport was all about, but by now I've been riding long enough to know a few things," he said.

"Huh. I thought you were a pro sponsored by Specialized," she blurted.

JD laughed, "That's generous of you. No. I do business with Specialized. Cycling is my hobby, not my job."

"So what do you do for work?" she cringed at the way the question came out so abruptly, but she was curious.

"Good question. I'm not sure you have enough time for me to answer that. What do you do, Mackenzie?"

"I'm in sales…" and then feeling like a fraud, added, "for now." She didn't want to pretend. JD seemed like a guy who respected honesty.

"For now? What do you mean by that?" JD inquired.

Mackenzie responded, "I don't think I'm cut out for sales." Then, wanting to impress him with her determined attitude, "I'm going to start looking for another job."

"Hmmm. Well, on Tuesday morning's ride, did the thought cross your mind that you weren't cut out to ride with this group?"

This guy doesn't sugarcoat anything, Mackenzie thought then asked, "How did you know that?"

"I've been riding long enough to know. And what made you show up this morning?" JD inquired.

Mackenzie responded, "You told me to show up. I wanted to try out what you taught me."

JD looked like he was considering his next words, "If there were a way for you to improve consistently, then would you be willing to take on a challenge?"

Mackenzie knew she could advance on her biking skills if she had the right coach. She nodded eagerly and said, "Absolutely."

JD wrote down a phone number on a napkin and asked, "Do you know of Bill Reichardt?"

Mackenzie was astonished at the mention of that name and squeaked out, "Bill Reichardt? 'I own the store' Bill Reichardt?"

JD chuckled, "That's the one."

Mackenzie's heart started pounding excitedly despite not understanding how Bill could help her with cycling, "Yeah, I just saw his commercial a few days ago! I didn't know that Bill used to be a cyclist! Wow, he's really done a lot in his life."

JD quickly understood her confusion and laughed, "Bill knows a little about everything, but he knows the most about business. This won't be a cycling talk. Call him and set up a meeting with him at Reichardt's Clothing Store. I'll let him know to expect your call. Bill still owns the store, but others work it. He has a fairly steady stream of people going in to talk with him."

Astonished that she was going to meet Bill Reichardt, she asked, "Are you sure he'll have time to talk with me?"

JD replied, "Bill will make time for anyone who wants to learn and grow. Bill realized that for a person to change his ways, that person needs to decide to change. 'There will be no change until the pain of change is less than the pain of staying the same.' That's his line. Where are you with your pain, Mackenzie?"

"In enough pain to be ready for change," she replied, surprising herself with the seriousness of her own tone.

JD paused and then continued, "Remember what you just said. When you meet Bill, he'll tell you about how he got started with the store. Make sure you take notes. Next Tuesday, meet me at 5:45 AM before the ride, here at the coffee shop, and we can debrief what you learned."

Mackenzie smiled genuinely. No one had ever opened a door

for her like this before, and she wasn't sure why JD would do this. But, at the moment, she didn't care why. *I get to meet Bill Reichardt!* She wasn't sure what he was going to tell her, but if he could own a store for decades, she wanted to hear whatever he had to say. She kept her excitement hidden and answered with seriousness, "Got it. Thanks, JD. I'll look forward to meeting Bill and talking to you on Tuesday."

A LOOK BACK
Chapter 7

Reichardt's Clothing Store was located in a quaint shopping center off 42nd Street. Mackenzie took one last look at herself in the reflection from the glass storefront, paying particular attention to her shirt and skirt. She had debated with herself about which top to wear, opting for her favorite that was the most fashionable, certainly received the most compliments, and was likely a little too low cut. Having gained a few pounds over the last two months, the skirt she wore was too tight and had inched its way up past her knees, but she thought that it still looked good on her. Mackenzie took one last deep breath and repeated to herself, "I am willing to take on the pain of change to get rid of the pain of staying the same."

A small bell rang as she entered the store. An older gentleman in a full dark gray suit, white collared button-down shirt and red tie greeted her with a gentle smile. "Good morning and welcome to Reichardt's. I don't believe I have had the pleasure of meeting you. I'm Henry, sales associate here at Reichardt's. May I help you find something for yourself or someone else today?" He offered his hand to her.

She felt like she stepped back in time. *Who greets someone at the door that way?* She started to stammer as she shook his hand, "Uh, hi Henry, I'm Mackenzie Jones...I'm, uh, I'm meeting with Mr. Reichardt this morning? Is he available?"

Henry replied, "Bill will make himself available if you have a meeting scheduled. I'll let him know you're here, Mackenzie Jones. Please make yourself comfortable and take a look around. He's talking with an old friend of his and usually takes a few minutes to finish up his conversations." He walked to the back of the store and disappeared.

Henry returned in less than a minute. "Bill will see you in five minutes. Have you talked with Bill before?"

She replied, "No, I've never met Mr. Reichardt. I've only seen him on TV. But, a man named JD told me to meet him."

"Ah, JD. JD Anderson, I presume?" Mackenzie nodded as Henry continued, "What a great man. I'm always eager to hear people's reaction when meeting him. What have you noticed about JD?"

Mackenzie thought about her answer. "He's a really strong cyclist!" she offered, and then feeling self-conscious for the shallowness of her response, added, "And he looks out for other people. Other than that, I don't know much about him. Do you know him well?"

Henry answered, "Observant. Yes, he does look out for others. And, yes, I do know JD. I've known him for years."

Henry had a gift of reading people and sensed that this young woman needed to know more, "Bill became like a dad to JD and coached him in the Little All-American Football League that Bill started way back. Tough childhood, tough kid. And a smart kid. He worked here during the summers in high school."

Mackenzie felt a kinship with anyone else who had a less than perfect childhood and responded, "I never would have guessed that JD had a tough childhood."

Henry nodded. "Bill picked up a lot of troubled kids from the

A LOOK BACK 33

street, put a uniform on their backs and gave them a new identity, through sport, which kept them out of trouble for a time. Some kids still found trouble, but many of them took a different path because they picked up what Bill gave them and literally ran in a different direction with it. JD was one of those kids."

Mackenzie didn't know how to respond. She wondered if JD somehow knew that she had a similar backstory with her own upbringing.

Henry continued, "JD learned a lot from Bill, added his own expertise to his craft and then started teaching others, including me. JD went on to earn a football scholarship at the University of Iowa and made quite a name for himself as a salesman after graduating."

Baffled, Mackenzie asked, "JD is in sales?"

Henry smiled, "Sure is. JD will tell you that everyone is in sales. All of the top salesmen in the Midwest have bought their suits here over the past decades, so I've met a lot of salesmen. JD is the greatest I've ever met; he's the best seller."

JD is the best seller? Of what? Mackenzie reprimanded herself for not knowing more about JD. The past few nights, she had read as much as she could find about Bill. There was so much to read that she didn't even think to research JD, let alone find out his last name. *At least I know his last name now*, she noted.

Henry paused and looked at her with a twinkle in his eyes, "Someone is looking out for you, Miss Mackenzie. JD is in a class all his own. And now you're about to meet his mentor, a man who has made a difference in a lot of people's lives. Bill may not be approved by all, but there is nothing dull about him. Be ready to listen. You'll be glad you did." Henry looked toward the back of the store.

Mackenzie followed his gaze and watched Mr. Bill Reichardt leaning heavily on his friend as they walked slowly toward them. With his balding crown and lumbering limp, he looked older than he did on TV. The deep worry lines across Bill's forehead and furrows on his face suggested that this was a man who would have a solemn view on life. That fit with the impression she had of him from his commercials.

Bill quipped a comment to his friend and they both laughed suddenly with an unrestrained burst of noise that reverberated off the wood-paneled walls. Mackenzie was surprised by the strength and levity in his laugh and reconsidered the somberness of Bill Reichardt as they finally made their way to the front of the store.

Bill looked at Mackenzie, smiled, elbowed his friend and said, "Randolph, I want you to meet Miss Mackenzie Jones. Mackenzie, this is Randy Duncan. Randy was the University of Iowa quarterback for two Rose Bowls, he's the most respected lawyer in the state, and he was the worst campaign manager the world has ever seen!" Bill deadpanned.

Randy replied, "Mackenzie, Bill ran for Governor of Iowa back in the 90s. His chance of winning that race was the same as an ice cube's chance in hell."

Bill retorted, "The only reason I got beat was because Duncan was my campaign manager!"

Randy guffawed and leaned in toward Mackenzie, "Even I didn't vote for Reichardt!" Randy handed Mackenzie the cane, "Here, take this so you can beat Bill over the head with it when he doesn't stop talking."

Randy laughed and shook Mackenzie's hand, saying goodbye. Mackenzie marveled at the exchange between the two men who clearly enjoyed a verbal sparring match. As if that were a normal way to say goodbye, Henry took Bill by the elbow, and they started walking slowly back to his office.

She followed Bill and Henry to the back of the store and studied her surroundings of elegantly displayed business suits of every shade of grey, navy, and black. A few brightly patterned jackets peppered other rows but looked to be there just for show and not to be taken seriously.

FIRST IMPRESSIONS
Chapter 8

As Henry gently helped Bill back to his desk, Mackenzie looked around at all of the framed pictures on the walls. The gallery boasted photos of Mr. Reichardt standing with a variety of well-dressed people, vintage football photos, as well as newspaper articles about juvenile delinquency and political elections. Finally, sticking out like a sore thumb was a life-sized, polyester moose-head which was mounted on the back wall above Bill's desk. On top of the moose head was a flat black hat with a golden fabric "I" logo sewed to the front. *What an interesting assortment decorating the walls,* Mackenzie noted.

Henry nodded to Mackenzie as he returned to the sales floor.

Mackenzie's palms were beginning to sweat, but she managed to extend her hand to say, "Mr. Reichardt, thank you for meeting with me, I truly appreciate it."

Bill reached out his hand to shake hers. His handshake was firm, and his eyes looked straight into hers as he said, "Mackenzie, call me Bill. JD told me you are eager to learn a few things. Let's start by working on your first impression."

Bill extended his hand to her again and she met it with hers as he said, "Your handshake is your second opportunity to build trust with whomever you are meeting. You look them in the eye, say their name with confidence, shake hands firmly, and disarm 'em with a smile." He beamed a toothy grin, and she couldn't help but smile back. He extended his arm towards her seat, and he labored to sit down in his chair.

"Your *first* opportunity in building trust is your clothing. What you wear is important. Mackenzie, the last time you saw the President of the United States on TV or online, what was the President wearing?"

Mackenzie was taken off-guard by his comment and immediately regretted what she chose to wear. "I don't remember, but I'm sure it was some sort of suit and tie."

"Exactly. It's planned that way. If you were attracted to something the President was wearing you'd be distracted from what the President was saying. The President wants you to listen to his words when he gives a speech, not to talk about his clothing. You choose what you wear so that you function, not your clothes."

Bill continued, "I realize that the women's clothing industry has spent billions of dollars marketing the latest fashions to make more money. Good for them. However, an individual businesswoman needs to decide what sort of message she wants to send by wearing the latest revealing fashions. Many women nowadays talk about how they should be able to wear what they want to wear and not be judged. The reality is, everyone is judged by what they wear. If a man wore a shirt with his top three buttons open, displaying his masculine chest at a business meeting, you wouldn't have a clue as to what he was saying, because all you would be thinking is, 'Man, that's a lot of chest hair!'" Bill shook his head.

Mackenzie sat, in frozen shock, between the shame she felt about her own low-cut top and the ridiculousness of the picture he painted of a man bearing his chest hair in a business meeting. She was torn between two opposite reactions. *How dare you say that!* And *You've got a point, there.*

She had agreed with plenty of blog articles about the need for women to bravely make a statement with feminine clothing instead of dressing like a man, but the contrast Bill gave caused her to rethink her opinion. She took a deep breath and, despite her wish to walk quickly out of the office, she chose to shift her shirt upwards. She fought the lump forming in her throat.

"If you can afford to talk about your clothes, like when you are out with your friends, then, by all means, wear clothes to talk about. Have fun with it! In business, though, you want what you're saying to be the focus instead of something you're wearing."

Bill's tone became gentle, "Mackenzie, it's important to learn that when we wear something distracting, it makes what we say much less efficient."

Mackenzie's mind recalled JD's similar description of her windbreaker jacket, how the wrong gear would make her work harder while making her much less efficient. She had never thought about how what she wore affected more than how she felt.

Bill continued, "Now, we've all been in a situation where what we're wearing affects us negatively. Sometimes we realize it on our own, and sometimes someone else makes us aware of it. How we react will determine if it changes us. I recall one particular situation where it certainly changed me."

Bill leaned back in his chair, relaxed. "You may know that I played football for the University of Iowa. In my senior year, I was named the Big Ten's Most Valuable Player. My Iowa football team didn't even win a conference game that year. Not one. But, somehow, the *Chicago Tribune* newspaper named me the Big Ten's MVP in 1951. I was to be honored with my photo on the front of the *Chicago Tribune*'s Sports Section and given a silver football trophy." Bill pointed to a framed newspaper article on the wall.

"I didn't own a suit at the time, but my coach told me I needed to wear one. They expected me to dress appropriately for the occasion. I would be representing the University of Iowa. It was my duty to dress respectfully. Coach found me a blue suit. It didn't fit, but it was my only option. I didn't own dress socks, so I stole some clean, white athletic socks from the locker room.

"I received that prestigious award wearing the tightest blue suit and white tube socks showing from beneath the short pant legs. I was directed to sit down after receiving the award, and my pants ripped at the rear seam."

Bill slapped his knee and bellowed, "Bahawhawhaw!"

Mackenzie managed an amused look, appreciating the story intended to lessen her humiliation.

Bill reverted back to his serious tone, "I was not the picture of dressing for success. That event made a crucial impression on me. I was there receiving the biggest award of my young life, but I wasn't feeling the esteem because I was thinking about my clothes, not the honor I was being given. That was my first big lesson in how what I wear, and how it fits, matters. I was embarrassed and decided that I would not put myself in a similarly humiliating situation ever again."

Bill placed his weighty hand on the desk, "So, Mackenzie, we've all had these moments. You can have a bad moment, but it doesn't make it a bad day. It's just a moment. And the key is to learn from the moments, both good and bad. After I have a bad moment in a day, I come into this office to take a look at that moose and that cap perched on top of it." He paused.

Mackenzie had regained her composure enough to ask, "Why is that?"

Bill answered, "My friend gave me that moose. I might tell you that joke someday. But, it's what is sitting on top of that moose that is most significant to me. The black cap with the gold capital "I" is why I'm here today. It's called an 'I-cap.' Do you want to know why that I-cap is so important?"

"Yes," Mackenzie replied while thinking, *I'll listen to anything that is not about what I'm wearing!*

Bill replied, "Good. I'd tell you about it whether you wanted to hear it or not. Hawhawhaw," he bellowed as he grinned from ear to ear, making Mackenzie smile along with him.

CLEAN SLATE
Chapter 9

Bill began, "This is the story that JD wants me to tell you. And the reason he wants me to tell you this story is that he has heard it hundreds of times. He didn't listen to it for entertainment's sake; he listened to it to learn from it. Over the decades of listening, thinking, and applying, JD extracted a set of Steps & Rules that resulted in his business success.

"That JD is a thinker. I never spent time reflecting on how or why Reichardt's was successful. I just did whatever seemed right at the time. Some of my ideas worked, others failed. But JD became a student of my life's stories and created his own successes while minimizing my many failures by applying his Steps & Rules.

"Developing quality, intentional, and practical Steps & Rules became essential to JD, and clearly communicating them to those he chose to mentor became non-negotiable. Most great salespeople have practiced their methods so long that their efforts become instinctual. These sales experts don't know how to explain their instincts to someone who is new to learning the process which is why so many up-and-coming sales people struggle to learn a process that should be easily understood, adaptable, and replicable. JD realized that the sales cycle is a complex process that can be made simple."

Mackenzie recalled JD saying that cycling was more complex than just jumping on a bike and pedaling. She also remembered thinking that if she could land a sales job with no experience, then she could conquer the simple act of selling. *Obviously, I have a lot to learn about both. I wonder if cycling and selling have more parallels.*

Bill continued, "Thankfully, this sales process can be made simple for you too. In order to do this, you will have to capitalize on your curiosity to follow a non-traditional approach, develop the discipline to embrace a tried and true process, and cultivate the perseverance to continually practice applying his Steps & Rules."

Mackenzie considered the requirements of curiosity, discipline, and perseverance. These were characteristics that could belong to anyone who was willing to put in the effort. She was willing and ready to learn.

Bill nodded as he saw her thinking about what he said, "So often in sales, we are expected to arrive at the destination, which often just looks like hitting a certain number, but rarely are we taught what roadblocks to expect or what curves and turns to anticipate. JD cared enough to document a process that guides young people on how to personalize interactions and establish trust so that success in relationships can correlate to success in business and sales and broader life.

"Mackenzie, I don't spend a lot of time with every person, so for JD to ask me to meet with you, he must have seen something in you. JD can sense and see more potential in people than they see in themselves. And he's out to prove it to you."

Mackenzie wasn't sure why JD would say that. She was

perplexed and intrigued. She sat up taller in her chair and leaned forward to listen.

Bill began, "And now, to give you a little history, a little background. It was 1953. I was serving at Bolling Air Force Base during the Korean War. My former Iowa football teammate and good friend, Bud Flood, and I had talked about opening up a sports shop. We knew we'd do fine because I was a football star and people wanted to buy things from a football star. Or, so we thought. To get started, Bud would manage the store, and I'd stay stationed in Washington, DC.

"We opened up 'Bill Reichardt and Bud Flood's Sports Shop' in Des Moines, Iowa, with $4,000 down for a bank loan. $4,000 was roughly half of my salary from playing football for the Green Bay Packers the year before.

"We didn't know how to bring people into the store, we didn't know anything about marketing, and we couldn't afford to advertise. We couldn't afford not to advertise, but we didn't know that then. Bud kept trying to bring the right equipment and sports clothing into the store to bring in more customers. We both thought that if my name wouldn't bring them in, then we needed to increase our supply of various equipment. Clothing and equipment manufacturers started to put inventory in the store on consignment, which means that we didn't have to pay for it until we sold it. In three years, we had over $70,000 worth of inventory in the store.

"In the middle of 1956, I was discharged from the Air Force and came back to Des Moines. I joined Bud at the store, and I was really impressed with the vast supply he had brought in on consignment. Sales still weren't paying all of the bills, but at least we had enough inventory to sell if customers walked in the door.

"Then a few weeks later at 4 AM one morning, I got a call. It was the police. The officer told me there was a robbery at the store. I immediately drove to the store. Bud was already there. The whole inventory was wiped out. Everything was gone. Everything. The robbers had posed as painters and convinced the overnight janitor that they were told to move everything out of the store so that they could paint the interior. The janitor helped them put every last item into their trucks, and no one stopped them. I was speechless."

Mackenzie shook her head in disbelief.

"I tried to look for the silver lining, and offered to Bud, 'Well, at least we have insurance.' 'Bill,' Bud told me as he shook his head, 'We have fire insurance. We don't have theft insurance; it was too expensive.'

"We were both so devastated. Bud and his wife had two babies at home. Sue and I also had two babies at home. My bank account only held a few thousand dollars. Suddenly, I was in debt over $70,000. This was back in 1956. That's more than a half million dollars today. We couldn't see any way out of it. People didn't just declare bankruptcy back then. We'd have to dig ourselves out of the mess.

"Bud went to get a few part time jobs in Des Moines. The only way I knew how to make money was to play football. I lined up a position to play for the Canadian professional football league in Vancouver. They told me I wouldn't get paid until I played all the exhibition games."

Bill leaned back in his chair, "They do things differently in Canada. They even play differently in Canada. They don't block for you on the kick off. Whoever is dumb enough to catch the ball gets totally slaughtered. On the first half of the last exhibition game, I caught the ball on the kick-off. My whole damn team just stood there and watched me get creamed. I was hit so hard by four guys that my head split wide open, someone kicked and chipped two of my teeth, and I was knocked out cold."

Bill shrugged, "Football is a violent sport. At the hospital, they gave me 19 stitches across my forehead and 17 across my nose. So, at that point, my face matched my financial situation. Totally broke! Hawhawhawhaw!" He bellowed as he slapped his knee. Although Mackenzie didn't understand why Bill thought this dismal description of his situation was funny, his hearty chuckles helped her to feel more at ease.

He continued, "I took the train back to Des Moines and walked into our empty store. The only thing left was this giant metal desk before me today and this chair that I'm sitting in. I just sat here, looking at the bare walls and thought, *where do I go from here?*"

Mackenzie shook her head again. *Yikes*, she thought, *I should not be complaining about my job.*

Bill continued, "I pulled out this middle desk drawer to see if there was even a scrap of paper and a pen left behind from the robbery. I needed to write things down to stop all the spinning in my head. There, shoved in the back of this drawer were ten black caps with a gold fabric letter "I" on them, the logo of the University of Iowa Hawkeyes. I had named these 'I-caps.'"

Bill tossed an I-cap to Mackenzie, and she caught it gingerly. The bold, golden "I" contrasted nicely from the black fabric. It wasn't her style, but it certainly made a statement.

Bill continued, "I thought these were going to be a popular item for University of Iowa football fans. I had Bud get them custom made two years prior after having what I thought was an epiphany as I observed the military uniform hats on the Air Force Base. The caps were sleek and had distinction. Like the caps on the Air Force Base branded you with your rank, these caps branded you as a fan of the University of Iowa.

"Our customers did not agree with me. Those I-caps cost $1.25 to make, and we had tried to sell them for $2.50 in the store. I had not sold a single I-cap in the two years we had them on the shelves — not one. The week before the robbery I finally took these I-caps off of the shelves. I tried giving them away to whomever I met in my office. I was told the I-cap wasn't their style. They all wore their fedoras when they occasionally attended Iowa football games. Two people accepted the hats with pity written on their faces. After a dozen more 'No, thank yous,' I shoved the remaining ten caps in the back of this drawer.

"Now, if you remember, my senior year was in 1951, when my University of Iowa football team didn't win a conference game. The store was robbed in 1956. I was broke, beat up, and all I had were these ten Iowa Hawkeye caps that I could barely give away."

Bill leaned forward in his chair, and looked seriously in Mackenzie's eyes, "When you get knocked down, it's okay to stay down for a moment and catch your breath. But, you don't do yourself or anyone else any good if you stay down. You gotta look up and get up.

"I had done that hundreds of times on the football field. This was real life in the business world now. So, I looked up and saw the empty walls around me. I decided that I had a clean slate. It was time to get up and move forward.

"I looked again at those I-caps in my hands. That gave me a focus. I remembered that the Iowa Hawkeyes were actually winning games that season in 1956 and would have a deciding game that next Saturday. Their record gave me hope that someone would see value in identifying with a winning team. I had hoped that, with a winning team, at least a few people would want those caps. I just had to go find those people.

"I called Bud and told him that I'd take the 10 caps down to the train depot on Saturday. In my day, the downtown train depot was a hub for Hawkeye fans to gather together and ride to away-games. Iowa would be playing Minnesota. Iowa was expected to lose big to Minnesota, but I thought that maybe someone would see at least a novelty value in an I-cap. I'd see if I couldn't sell them for a dollar. Bud said he'd go with me.

"At the train depot, I stood there with one I-cap on my head and nine hats in my hands. A very well-dressed man, who had clearly started the morning with a few gin and tonics, saw my hat and shouted, 'Hey, young fella! What's that hat you're wearin'?'

I immediately put one of the I-caps in his hands, "This is the official University of Iowa football fan cap. It's called the I-cap."

The man pursed his lips and furrowed his brow, 'I've been going to Iowa football games for a decade, and I've never seen anything like this. How much ya want for these caps?'

As I was about to tell him one dollar, Bud walked behind the guy and signaled me with four fingers up. I was thinking, *There is no way we're gonna sell these for four dollars, but what do we have to lose?*

'Four dollars,' I told him.

'Four dollars. Each?' the drunk man asked.

'Yes,' I said, without wavering.

'I'll take them all,' said the dapper drunk man as he reached into his pocket.

'All of them?' I stammered, immediately regretting opening my mouth.

'Did I stutter? Yeah, all of them. The Hawk Club is going to get a kick out of these. I want them all.'

"I couldn't even remember what four dollars times ten hats equaled. I've never been good at math," Bill shrugged at Mackenzie.

"The guy already had two twenty dollar bills out of his wallet. 'Forty dollars. Thank you.' I said, stunned that one customer bought all ten caps, on the spot, for four times what I wanted to ask.

"Bud and I couldn't believe it. We sped back to the store, and I called up the hat manufacturer in St. Louis. We had sold fedoras in the store from that hat manufacturer, but not enough to cover the losses from the robbery. I begged him to send us

500 I-caps. He said no. We couldn't pay their consignment bill from the robbery, and he wasn't about to lose another $600 to cover the I-cap shipment. I told him the whole story, and he found empathy for me. He said, 'If you can guarantee the bill for the caps, then I'll send them.'"

I-CAPS

Chapter 10

Bill continued, "My mind was racing. That first customer said he knew that his Hawk Club alumni friends would want an I-cap. At that moment, I knew in my gut that I could sell the I-caps. Nothing was going to stop me. I immediately called the bank who loaned me money to help open the store. I didn't know the first banker I was speaking to, but I was in such a rush and thought that I would get a yes. The first banker said, 'I'm sorry, Mr. Reichardt. The bank can't lend you any more money with the debt you have right now.'

"Thankfully, I remembered that my wife's friend from the University of Iowa was the wife of a young bank manager, Crawford Hubbell. I asked if my call could be transferred to Mr. Hubbell, and it was.

"I recalled our meeting at a cocktail party months prior. Although Crawford had gone to Harvard and was cut from a very different cloth than me, we found common ground with sports and serving in the military. We didn't talk much about our time in the service because we both had lost a lot of friends. So, instead, Crawford and I had a good time trading college sports stories. He was tall and slight, suited to play golf. My golf swing looked more like a baseball hack, and he admitted he could barely catch a football, so we shared laughs and stories from the green and on the field.

"After a few pleasantries over the phone, I asked if I could have a meeting with him. He obliged, and I immediately drove over to meet Crawford. He walked out of his office, greeted me, and gave me his condolences about my store's robbery. He was direct and had clearly been told by the other banker about my asking for the $600 loan because the next thing he said was, 'Bill, I'm sorry, but I have to agree with my colleague. Right now, you are too much risk to take on with the loss of your entire store inventory. The bank cannot offer you another loan.'

"I couldn't afford a no. I needed a yes. And fast. So I used the only play I had. I went back to our common ground of sports. I told him, 'Crawford, in 1951, it was my last year to play at the University of Iowa. Our record in the Big Ten was 0-5. We did not win a game. My last game playing for the University of Iowa was against the Fighting Irish at Notre Dame. We were expected to lose by at least 14 points. It was a non-conference game, so it didn't matter to our Big Ten standings, but it mattered to me. I was not going to let our team lose. In that game I had the team doc give me 21 shots of Novocain. Coach didn't know about it. I wanted to do it. That's how important the game was to me.'

"Then I told him, 'Crawford, I was in pain. I needed to get past the pain to carry that ball to where it needed to go. I'm coming to you today for a different kind of shot. You can give me this shot to win.' I looked him straight in the eye and said, 'I. Will. Not. Lose.'

"He hesitated, so I kept talking. I told him about selling the I-caps that morning and the hat manufacturer's deal. I felt like he wanted to help but needed more assurance, 'Crawford, if there were a way for me to guarantee that I will sell all five hundred hats, then would you be willing to lend me $600?'

"He said, 'Bill, I'll tell you what. There's a much better likelihood that you'll sell these caps if Iowa beats Minnesota. If the Hawks win today, then I will personally lend you enough money to pay the invoice.'

"We shook hands, and I went straight to the nearest Catholic Church to light a candle for the Hawkeyes to pull off this upset.

"Iowa won that game against Minnesota, 7-0. It was nothing short of a miracle.

"We got the money and the 500 hats just in time to ride out to Iowa City for the next game against the Ohio State Buckeyes, another game we were predicted to lose, but optimistic to win. I walked to my old U of I fraternity house, got the guys hyped on this I-cap and told them that I'd give them a quarter for every cap they sold. I picked the 10 guys I thought were the most hungry to make some money. At the stadium gates, before the game began, we sold all of them. In a huge upset, the Iowa Hawkeyes beat the Ohio State Buckeyes 6-0.

"At the end of the game, the stadium crowd rushed onto the field, wrenched both of Iowa's steel goal posts from their moorings in eight feet of concrete. Echoes of 'I-O-Wa-Wa! I-O-Wa-Wa!' were heard throughout Iowa City, as the power plant's steam whistle blasted again and again. Fans were delirious.

"The Iowa Hawkeyes would be going to the Rose Bowl for the first time ever in the history of the University.

"This was it — the biggest college game of the year. Things were really coming together. The next weekend, Crawford rolled over the loan, and we took 2,000 caps to Iowa City for the next game against the Fighting Irish of Notre Dame. It was a big risk to take that many caps to a non-conference game, but I had to bet big that the frenzied fans were eager to show their support for their winning Hawkeyes, that they'd part with their hard-earned money. Fans at the gates were clamoring to buy these I-caps. We didn't have enough supply to meet the demand. It was clear that people wanted to be identified as an Iowa Hawkeye fan.

"In December, Sue and I went to every party we could get an invite to, snuck into a few uninvited and we started rubbing elbows with as many socialites as we could. We took I-caps in the trunk of our car, wherever we went, selling over 1,000 caps at different events. I recruited even more fraternity brothers on Iowa's campus, who sold over 3,000 caps at pep rallies.

"We felt the Hawkeye fever rising and organized a Hawkeye Rose Bowl train to take fans from Des Moines to Pasadena. Sue and I rolled out the red carpet for Crawford and his wife, Corinne, who paved the way for us. We filled those trains with people for the Rose Bowl game against Oregon State to be played on New Year's Day, 1957. More importantly, we took duffel bags stuffed with 15,000 I-caps. We organized about 50 people to sell caps, still paying them a quarter per cap sold.

"We sold all 15,000 of those I-caps by kick-off." Bill leaned back, clapped his hands and howled a big belly laugh.

"Wow. That's amazing," Mackenzie marveled.

Bill replied, "Yes, it was amazing. In total, we sold over 20,000 caps for $4 each that year. Selling those I-caps gave us the momentum that saved my business."

VISION

Chapter 11

Bill leaned forward towards Mackenzie. "Do you know what's even more amazing than selling 20,000 I-caps in three months back in 1956?" Bill paused, and Mackenzie shook her head. "It's that more than one person bought an I-cap in the first place. The concept of the I-cap was way ahead of its time."

"How so?" Mackenzie asked.

Bill continued, "Think about watching a college or professional football game on TV today. What are the fans wearing?"

"Team colors, team jerseys, the team logo on their shirts," Mackenzie answered.

"At a minimum," Bill retorted. "If the fans are not wearing their team's colors, logos and mascots all over their bodies, some don't consider them a real fan. Nowadays, there are even Green Bay Packers fans that wear giant wedges of cheese-shaped foam as hats. As tacky as that may be, fans high-five each other with a great sense of belonging.

"That was not the case back in the 1950s. With what people wear to sporting events today, it's hard to imagine it being so different. In 1956, men spectators watching a game in the stadium dressed up in a sport coat, tie, freshly shined shoes, and a fashionable fedora hat. Women sports spectators wore conservative skirts and cardigan sweaters. If fans were feeling spirited, they would wave pennants, which were felt triangles on popsicle sticks decorated with the name of the school and logo. Here's a photo of some fans traveling to the Rose Bowl."

Bill handed Mackenzie an old photo showing University of Iowa football fans waiting for the train heading to Pasadena. She noticed a few fellows wearing I-caps and everyone was dressed conservatively.

"That was the extent of the logo's presence. The athletes' uniforms were literally just a uniform. The jerseys and helmets boasted no logos - not even the name of their school - just the school color and dark block-typed numbers. The only time a college athlete would show off their team's logo was after they earned the right to wear a Letter Jacket. You had to earn your Letterman's Club access through blood, sweat, and tears. It was…" Bill trailed off as he was interrupted by Henry knocking on the open door.

Henry said, "Bill, sorry to interrupt. Mr. Woodlawn wanted to tell you hello as he picked up his new suit and that he's sorry he missed you. And, Mr. Cooper is here with his grandson. He said you told him to bring his grandson, Tyrone, in to talk with you."

Bill responded, "I sure did. Yes, tell him to bring in Tyrone in two minutes."

Bill turned back to Mackenzie and continued, "Mackenzie, I'll wrap this up and leave you with a question to discuss with JD." He paused. "Branding and merchandising college or professional sports gear didn't hit the mainstream until the early 1970s. No one wore logos back in the 1950s. There was an unwritten dress code, and people did not deviate from that dress code. I want you to think about that. And I want you to think about the following question: How was I able to transform a product, with no apparent value in the marketplace, into the hottest selling item of the season?"

Mackenzie nodded her head. "That's a great question. I will definitely think about that and talk with JD about it. Thank you so much for your time, Bill."

"Mackenzie, it's been a pleasure. Next time I'd like to hear what you've learned. Come back in to talk with me in a few weeks."

Mackenzie walked out and smiled at the well-dressed businessman with his teenage grandson. The businessman smiled back politely. The teenage grandson didn't even look up; he was focused on the hole he was digging with his shoe as he kicked into the burgundy carpet.

PART TWO

Steps & Rules

THE FIRST LESSON
Chapter 12

Mackenzie arrived at the Dynamo Coffee Shop early on Tuesday morning and anxiously reviewed her notes from Bill's story. Just as she worked hard to show her favorite professors in college that she could master the material, she wanted to impress JD with her critical thinking and preparation. Perhaps she would bring up a point to give JD a new perspective. *After all*, she thought, *the marketplace has changed considerably since the 1950s.*

JD walked into the coffee shop a few minutes later and was welcomed like a local celebrity. After he had shared small talk with the handful of his fellow early-bird patrons, JD sat down across from Mackenzie, right on time for their scheduled meeting. "Good morning, Mackenzie. We don't have much time before the ride, so let's get right to the point. What did you take away from Bill's stories?"

Mackenzie was ready. "Bill suggested we discuss how he was able to transform a product, with no apparent value in the marketplace, into the hottest selling item of the season."

"Sounds like a good place to start. What did you come up with?" JD asked.

Mackenzie had rehearsed what she wanted to tell JD and began, "After considering a number of answers, I think these are my top two lessons learned:

1. Bill positioned himself in the optimal place to sell his product.
2. Bill moved quickly with a few lucky breaks. With the right timing, the right people said 'Yes.' He used his early victories to build the momentum needed to sell more I-caps."

Mackenzie paused, anticipating JD's affirmation for the brilliant way she boiled down the main points of Bill's story. She had rehearsed her reasoning behind each point but first wanted to present them simply to enhance her logic.

JD nodded and said, "Your first point is good. Positioning is very important, and we will talk about that later." He paused, considering how to proceed, "Your second point doesn't quite hit the mark, but it is what most non-salespeople think is the reason for success...luck. It is not luck!"

Mackenzie sat up straighter to hide the discouragement she felt as he called her a non-salesperson.

JD continued, "The harder you work at putting certain Steps & Rules into place, the luckier you get! What looks like luck to the untrained eye is really a systematic approach to the sales process."

JD leaned forward and lowered his voice, "It's all about... favorable access."

Her disappointment turned to intrigue as she remembered that 'favorable access' was the term Luke had mentioned when he invited her to the cycling group. "Favorable access," she repeated. "I'm not sure what you mean."

"Let's go back to Bill's story," JD said. "You see, Reichardt's was the first retailer in the country to distribute apparel with a

University logo embedded on the clothing. Bill's University of Iowa I-cap introduced a complete direction change to what football fans wore to games. Being the first to move a new product or concept is often the hardest uphill climb. If you study successful leading edge products, whether in 1950s apparel or today's disruptive technologies, you'll find the importance of having the right access to gain sales. You can have the greatest product, the smartest CEO, top notch IT, HR, and accounting, but without sales, nothing else matters. And without the right access, favorable access, you will have no sales."

JD gave her a half-smile, "But you won't find that information in a book. People often won't admit who opened the door for whom. Instead, we read stories of how a lone entrepreneur, in his or her stroke of genius, created a product or a concept that everyone suddenly wanted. But what was happening behind the scenes? That entrepreneur was creating demand-pull through favorable access."

There was the other term that Luke had mentioned. *Demand-pull*. The way JD said the two terms with the notion of opening doors made her recall the old, worn adage which gave her confidence that she had solved a riddle. She smiled triumphantly, "Ok, so you're saying, it's not what you know, it's who you know. Right?"

"Nope. It's not who you know. It's who knows you and trusts you or your product," JD replied.

Mackenzie slumped.

JD continued, "Bill didn't know what favorable access was either, at the time he was building it. But, before we talk about favorable access, we need to talk about general access. Too many people skip the first step and try to bulldoze through the process."

JD placed his pointer finger in the air and said quietly, "The first step is very important and you should not skip this. Step 1 in the sales process is: Understand your general access."

STEP 1: *Understand your general access.*

JD continued, "General access is when we know who is in our suspect pool. Most amateur salespeople never spend the front-end time really working through the suspect pool for their specific product; instead, like an amateur cyclist, they make random exaggerated pushes, thinking that effort expended anywhere in the race will drive them to the finish line in first place.

"If an organization or a sales team spends a disproportionate amount of time in the first six months clearly defining and understanding their suspect pool, their general access, they would be much more efficient in the next six months than with random cold calls in the marketplace. Organizations and their sales management rarely know the difference between a suspect and a prospect. They lump all suspects and prospects into the same category and subsequently miss the larger opportunities.

"Suspects are people who we have identified as having a high probability of wanting or needing our product. Once we have a large suspect pool, we then need to turn them into prospects. That is the difference between general access, people we know, versus favorable access, people who know us and our product. Step 2 in the sales process is: Develop a plan to gain favorable access."

STEP 2: *Develop a plan to gain favorable access.*

JD continued, "There is a lot of work required to move from general access to favorable access. You have to earn the opportunity for favorable access. When our suspects know us and trust us, our company, our product and/or our sales associates, that's when we have gained favorable access."

Mackenzie was impressed with JD's explanations and she responded, "That makes sense. No one has ever explained suspects and prospects to me like that. I want to make sure I get this right. I have general access with people that I have identified who may want or need my products. And you call them suspects, right?"

"That's correct," JD answered.

Mackenzie continued, "And you want to move your suspects to prospects. You define that as gaining favorable access?"

"That's correct." JD summarized, "And the simple difference between suspects and prospects is that, first, you know them and second, you want them to know you and trust you; whether it's you, your company or your product."

"Okay, I think I get it. Moving from general access to favorable access is the same thing as moving suspects into prospects, right?" Mackenzie asked.

"Exactly. Access is achieved sometimes by association, sometimes by a lot of strategic work and most of the time through a combination of both. Once you have favorable access, it's your job to build upon it and improve the relationship."

Mackenzie felt like she was learning the pieces but still couldn't see how Bill used favorable access selling that first I-cap. *Bill didn't know his first customer at all!* She was impatient for the answer, so she ventured, "JD, where did favorable access come into play with the I-cap?"

JD, sensing that she was fixated on the minutiae instead of the bigger picture, responded, "I'm going to have you think about your own question instead of telling you the answer. But what I will say right now is that favorable access can be created for you, your company, or your product."

Mackenzie felt herself get restless. She needed practical

answers to tell her how Bill moved from general access to favorable access so that she could apply the lesson in her job.

JD sensed her tension and knew she would need to wrestle with her questions in order to understand it better, so he added, "I learned many lessons from Bill's failures and successes and then took the time to see the patterns in order to develop and implement what I call the '8 Steps of the Sales Process.'"

Mackenzie yearned for a full set of logical steps to follow and asked, "Can you tell me what the other 6 steps are right now?"

"Nope. And there are also '8 Rules of the Paceline,' so to speak." JD looked at the time. "Right now it's time to roll on this bike ride."

The bike ride? I don't care about this bike ride! Mackenzie tried not to plead, "JD, can you just quickly tell me the rest of the steps and rules this morning? I really need to know how to turn things around at work. A bike ride is not going to change anything for me."

JD calmly replied, "One ride certainly won't change anything for you. Each ride where you challenge yourself to see beyond yourself, you will broaden your perspective. This ride is more important than you know." Then he backed out his chair, stood up and stretched his arms on the way to the door. He didn't look back.

Mackenzie remained seated, confused by JD's words. Whenever she had asked her college professors to explain a vague point in their lesson, they usually obliged and explained it step by step. JD's response was: "This ride is more important than you know." *What was that supposed to mean?* She didn't have time for talking around in circles. She needed practical advice. Now.

After a few deep breaths, she decided that she had two choices. She could forget this nonsense or seek the answers. She remembered that Bill told her to return to the store and tell him what she learned. Knowing that she did want to follow through and have something worthwhile to say to him, she knew she couldn't return with, 'Well, Bill, I learned that it's about favorable access.' And then fake her way through the rest of the conversation. *Same trick, different day.*

Mackenzie decided that it was worth it to seek the answers to this favorable access concept.

"STEPS" OF THE SALES PROCESS

Step 1: Understand your general access.
Step 2: Develop a plan to gain favorable access.

TREE BRANCH
Chapter 13

As Mackenzie tried to think about how someone could move from general access to favorable access, she glanced outside to see that a large cycling group had already gathered. It looked like the leader had already given the day's route. Her thoughts quickly pivoted back to the ride. She exited the shop and silently hoped to recognize a few of the women from the last ride.

She vaguely recognized one woman and was about to attempt an introduction of herself when she felt a tap on her shoulder. Just as Mackenzie turned, a familiar voice shouted, "Well, lookee here! Someone is trying her spin techniques outside of the cycling lab!"

"Lisa!" Mackenzie wanted to give her spin instructor a hug but wasn't sure Lisa liked hugs. Instead, she said, "You have no idea how happy I am to see you!"

"Likewise, my friend. So, how are you doing on the open road? A bit different than in the spin room, huh?"

"Ha! I'd say. The Sweeper had to save me on my first ride. But I'm getting a little better each ride."

Lisa snorted a laugh, "Well, it can only get better from there, huh? Knowing you, it won't take long for you to get in gear. So, have you met any of the other riders here?"

Mackenzie shook her head, "Not really."

"Well, let's fix that." In her coaching voice, Lisa hollered to the group around her, "Hey, everyone! I want to introduce one of my best spin students to you. The power output on this woman is wicked. I've just decided that Mackenzie is going to sit-in today, so let's show her how this works, shall we?!"

Mackenzie didn't understand where she would be 'sitting,' but nodded to play along. They rolled their bikes to the side of the group and Lisa spoke quietly, "You know we ain't here for a picnic. We're going to ride hard. By now, you've probably realized that there's a big difference between indoor and out. Have you learned how to draft?"

Mackenzie nodded, "I think so."

"Good," Lisa acknowledged. "Whatever you do, don't lose the wheel in front of you. You have to align with the wheel in front of you."

Mackenzie remembered that JD had told her the exact same thing. *There must be some kind of beginner handbook for cycling somewhere that I need to read,* she thought.

Lisa continued, "When everyone buys in to the formation, then we can build the best paceline. That's the biggest difference between spin class and the road. Out here, once we align in the paceline, we create team efficiencies in both energy and speed by riding in the draft of other riders. Not all riders have the same strength or endurance, but each member contributes towards the good of the team. In our race paceline, key riders take turns pulling the group. In our practice pacelines, each rider takes a turn rotating through to pull the group. The paceline pulls the team to get better, together." Lisa then turned to the group, waved her arm forward and shouted to the crowd, "It's time to ride! Let's roll, Dynamo!"

Lisa rolled her bike through the crowd, and Mackenzie

followed, watching the grins and happy exchanges between her and the others. Mackenzie smiled at her good luck of knowing Lisa. The other riders greeted Mackenzie with an enthusiasm she hadn't experienced since she was winning points for her college track team. Even the woman with the blue sunglasses slapped her on the back and gave her a thumbs up. Today, with Lisa's reassuring introduction, Mackenzie was somehow part of the club.

As Mackenzie observed the crowd, she noticed that many of the cyclists wore matching blue, white, and black gear. 'Dynamo Coffee' was written across their backsides with a logo of three lines converging to one. Despite the large lettering, she hadn't paid attention to the name until Lisa yelled out, "Let's roll, Dynamo!"

She quickly asked Lisa, "Does Dynamo Coffee sponsor the cycling group?"

"They do now. We used to be called something else and had a different meet-up spot. The Dynamo owner knew someone in our group and started offering half-priced coffee before 6 AM, so we started meeting here. We then hooked him up with a jersey manufacturer and helped design the kit. This shop is kinda our Clubhouse; there isn't a time, day or night, that you won't find a half a dozen or more members hanging out here. And, I gotta admit, I like the name."

Mackenzie agreed that it was a great name. With the feeling of being included, she wanted to be all in. She wanted the gear and would figure out how to pay for it later.

As they started to ride, Mackenzie followed whatever Lisa told her to do. Lisa rode next to her for the first few miles to make sure she was comfortable with her bike handling skills in a group, "Today, you're going to sit-in. That's the nice way of saying that you'll be a 'wheel-sucker.' Wheel-suckers are exactly what they sound like. They suck someone else's draft. They don't contribute. Normally, we don't allow wheel-suckers, even in the practice group. We make everyone contribute, even if it's for five seconds of pulling up front. As I said earlier, we pull each other to go faster, together. But, I'm giving you permission today to peel off without pulling for the rest of us because I want you to experience this group's dynamics and not get left behind. Next practice ride, no wheel-suckers."

"Got it. Thanks, Lisa," Mackenzie replied.

Lisa nodded, "Now, when drafting, your main job is to align with the wheel in front of you and hold your line. You have to look beyond the wheel in front of you to see what's coming up. Positioning is critical. Keep the right distance behind the wheel so that you don't overlap their wheel and cause yourself or anyone else to crash. Here, watch me."

Mackenzie observed the wheel distance, her eyes looking ahead. "Also, I decided five seconds ago to nickname you Z. Mackenzie's just too long," Lisa remarked. Mackenzie didn't care what Lisa called her; she was just happy to be known. "So, Z, go ahead and work your way behind Brenda, our Bren-in-blue sunglasses and blue helmet. Roll back when she does. Make sure to watch, listen and anticipate the other riders' movements."

Lisa was right. The ride was no picnic. Even in the draft, she had to push and pull hard to keep up. They were riding fast, and it appeared that each person took about thirty seconds in the lead, then rotated off, at least until the hills. On the hill climbs, the stronger riders went to the front, and the rest just tried to hang on.

Mackenzie had to adjust frequently in order to keep the same pace. A few times she lost her spacing and had to pull and push hard to get back into position. There was not a lot of verbal communication because they were winded, so body language took over as the communication mode. An elbow flick meant that the next person in the paceline was to take the lead. She had been so self-conscious on her other rides that she hadn't taken the time to really observe the group dynamics.

As the paceline hit a groove during a long straightaway and Mackenzie relaxed a bit more, she was in awe of the pace and how the paceline worked together. She noticed the speed and the relative ease of their team dynamics. She was also astonished by the difference she felt being invited into this group instead of hanging off the back, like an unwanted guest.

This discovery hit her like an unexpected tree branch hanging over the trail. *That's the power of favorable access,* she thought to herself. Two days prior, when she asked Bren-in-blue if she could join her, she was met with rejection. But this day was different because Lisa introduced her in a meaningful way. Lisa was a respected leader, and the members of the group trusted her recommendations.

Because of Lisa's favorable access and her approval of my power output, my status was immediately elevated from 'another suspect rider' to 'prospect who can contribute' to the group, Mackenzie's thoughts fired. *It would have taken me months to gain favorable access using my own techniques! This favorable access thing might actually work.* She began to understand how the ride could be more important than she originally thought. *But,* she thought, *I still don't understand how this applies to Bill's story or my own work situation. I'll just have to trust that JD knows what he's teaching.*

POSITIONING
Chapter 14

She could feel the rhythm of her own pedal cycle. She pushed with one leg while she pulled with the other. Push, pull. Push, pull. She focused on her positioning where she felt more pull of the draft and resumed pushing and pulling on her pedals. She found it was easier to complete the full push-pull cycle when she could connect to the pull of the draft. She felt less pressure on her legs, felt an ease of her breathing, and felt an increase of the group energy when she kept in stride. She looked ahead of the rider in front of her and got better at predicting the speed changes and avoiding the occasional bumps in the road.

If only my co-workers and I could work together like this paceline, she thought. Instead, they worked independently and were pitted against each other, as she and others fell off the back with no Sweeper. "This ride is more important than you know." JD's words echoed in her mind. *Was favorable access somehow connected to group dynamics? Could drafts be present in the workplace?* The thought struck her. If there was a draft in the workplace, she didn't know where to find it, but she knew she needed it.

In this second moment of favorable access epiphany,

Mackenzie decided that she would find JD again after the ride. The rest of the ride was a blur, and she made her way back to the coffee shop, scanning the cyclists for The Sweeper. She saw him rolling his bike to his car. She ran up to him and blurted, "It has to do with the draft, right?"

JD turned and nodded. "So the bike ride made you think about the difference between your solo effort, speed, and energy as compared to embracing the draft, a powerful pull, from a group. Very good."

Yes, thought Mackenzie and aloud she said, "So, does favorable access make someone buy a product?" Mackenzie asked, hoping there was some sort of connection.

JD answered, "As you know, when you're in the draft, you still have to do the work, think, respond, and reposition yourself, but the draft does make the overall ride more effective. Favorable access makes the next Steps of the sales process more effective. Favorable access, by itself, does not make a sale. But, your favorable access connection gives you direct access to the leveraging power of the sales process system."

Something about that last sentence reminded her of something someone had said, but she couldn't quite place it. *Maybe JD said that earlier,* she answered herself.

He continued, "As you'll recall, Bill could barely give his I-cap away to his regular customers, those with whom he had favorable access, just weeks before his first I-cap sale. In fact, Bill had ten of those I-caps sitting in his Reichardt's Sports Shop for two years, gathering dust, like most of the other inventory in the store. Bill originally thought he was going to sell his sports inventory, including those caps, because his name was known as a famous University of Iowa Hawkeye football player.

"Bill thought his name automatically gave him favorable access. However, when Bill played college and pro football, his media exposure was much more limited than college or professional athletes today. As Bill realized with his poorly performing

Sports Shop, fame is fleeting. Bill needed something stronger than former fame to pull the customers into the store and what he was selling needed to fill a deeper need in order to make a sale.

"Once Bill returned to the store after serving with the Air Force, he saw that Bud had acquired a great supply of sports inventory. Bill's response was to immediately push this supply within the sports shop and to push his name, while he was at it. Bill's supply-push gave him an opportunity to meet and understand his suspects. He supply-pushed into general access of his suspects.

"Let me pause here and explain the difference between what I call 'supply-push' and 'demand-pull' in sales. A push feels forced. When starting out any relationship, you often have to push a little. You have to push to meet someone new. You have to push to put yourself into position. However, once you get into position, you need to back off the push and mentally switch gears to achieve the pull.

"An amateur salesperson pushes to get into position, but never switches gears. That salesperson continues to try to push you into the sale. When a customer gets pushed towards the sale, the customer starts to push back. Many customers who are 'sold' by being pushed into the sale have some underlying buyer's remorse and will not be fully satisfied.

"A pull feels different. A pull is an attracting force that draws you into a particular direction. When your prospect is pulled it is because you have created a demand for you, your product or service, and the prospect decides to go along. A sophisticated salesperson creates a demand-pull for the product and then invites you to buy.

"To further illustrate this, let's use a biking analogy. Think back to your last ride where you were all alone, pushing those pedals as hard as you could to catch up with the pack. You were hurting and not making much progress. Now, think back to when I told you to 'align with the wheel in front of you.' You were pulled into the draft. Think about the difference in your effort and your speed between a push and a pull. When you position yourself favorably in a group with a pull, you allow yourself to use the paceline power of those around you.

"When you position yourself to use the pull-power of those around you or your product, then you have what we call 'alignment' in sales. Alignment pulls a customer toward a person or product and opens the door to the next step. The more alignment you have, the more demand-pull you'll have. The more pull you have, the easier the ride is towards the finish line. The more demand-pull for your product or service, the more easily the sale is finalized."

Mackenzie nodded along with these analogies. He was using a lot of terms in ways she hadn't heard before, and she was seeing the bigger picture, but all of the terms were getting jumbled in her head. Alignment, favorable access, demand-pull. This alignment term was new but seemed self-explanatory. The idea of favorable access was making sense, but demand-pull still remained elusive so she asked, "JD, could you explain demand-pull another way? I don't fully understand that term."

"You bet. I'm sure you took some sort of economics course in college and likely learned the terms 'supply and demand.' Do you remember how to define them?"

Mackenzie perked up at the idea of recalling terms she knew confidently, "Supply is defined as 'the quantity of an item in the market for purchase.' The economics definition of demand is: 'the consumer's desire and willingness to pay a price for a specific good or service.'"

"Excellent," JD encouraged. "So, we know that Bill had a small supply of ten caps. Now, remember that Bill always had a small supply. So, which factor changed?"

Mackenzie guessed the obvious answer, "Demand."

"Yes," JD agreed. "And demand is the customer's desire and

willingness to pay a price for a specific good or service. Bill's first customer was certainly willing to pay as we saw with the twenty dollar bills flying out of his wallet and he had the desire to do so. But what caused his desire?"

"The customer said he had been to the Iowa football games for over a decade and that was the first time he had ever seen an I-cap," Mackenzie asserted.

JD dubiously probed, "So, you think that Bill's supply-push of his new product into the customer's vicinity caused the customer's desire?"

Mackenzie added quickly, "And the customer said he wanted to show it off to his alumni group."

"Now we're getting somewhere," JD observed. "First, Bill's supply-push positioned the I-cap in front of a customer base that already had favorable access with the "I" logo. These fans knew the "I" stood for the University of Iowa. Then something about the I-cap pulled the customer's thoughts towards the upcoming rally with his alumni group. What caused that pull?"

Mackenzie admitted, "I'm not sure."

"What you aren't thinking about are the behind-the-scenes forces at work. The University of Iowa had spent decades marketing that "I" logo, creating awareness of the university. The general marketing for the University of Iowa created favorable access for that logo. The "I" logo went from being unknown to known and trusted.

"The branding and advertising of the "I" logo on the college campus also gave the students and alumni a common connection and sense of loyalty toward one another and the brand, thereby creating a demand-pull towards the logo. The Iowa football team was on a winning streak which increased the demand-pull to be identified with the team and connected closer to the "I" logo. One alumnus saw that this I-cap could align him with that demand-pull; the I-cap could make him the talk of a group full of favorable access, his alumni group, at a pre-game rally."

JD summarized, "To put it simply, favorable access opens the door between you and your prospect; demand-pull increases the desire of your prospect to move through the door. When I say 'you' here, I mean you, your product, or your company."

Mackenzie nodded and repeated, "So, favorable access gives you a better opportunity to create demand-pull. Demand is a prospect's desire and willingness to pay a price, and the pull is an attracting force that moves the prospect further along in the process. Demand-pull."

JD agreed, "You're getting it. When you as the salesperson can create a feeling in the prospect where the prospect starts to drive the sales process forward, you'll have demand-pull selling your product for you.

"It's just like how we increase momentum on the bike. We push and pull. Push against the pedal on the downstroke, pull the pedal towards yourself on the upswing. You can create momentum by just using the clunky push stroke. However, the fluid push and pull strokes create a stronger full circle momentum. The full circle momentum combined with the draft-pull created by you and others creates the most powerful demand-pull momentum."

She felt the power behind these terms. But she couldn't shake the gnawing feeling in her stomach and her skepticism rising, *this all sounds really good in theory but would it actually work in the real world?* Before she could filter her thoughts, she tested, "JD, this sounds like it worked in Bill's story, but as you said, his product had an established favorable access through the recognition of the "I" and demand-pull through the university's branding. What about something that doesn't have that established favorable access or demand-pull?"

JD stated, "You asked that question for a reason. Why are you asking that question?"

Mackenzie needed him to understand her dire circumstances at work, "My product doesn't have favorable access or demand-pull and my product isn't as simple. I have to educate people about my product and how to use it because it's software, not hardware, and certainly not tangible apparel. My product doesn't automatically tap into the team spirit of a loyal fan or any inherent sense of belonging. I'm not riding on amped up emotions with the pull towards a winning team. I'm at the wrong train station going in the wrong direction...and I'm late! I have to validate my numbers now!" Mackenzie immediately regretted how she increased her volume on the last sentences, making her sound frantic. She softened, "JD, how do I, someone who is totally new in sales, position myself to achieve favorable access and create demand-pull for the product I'm trying to sell?"

JD gave her a gentle and knowing look, "Right now, you're in a push mentality. You have to switch gears and either find or create a pull. But to do that, you need Rule 2: Go slow to go fast."

RULE 2: Go slow to go fast.

Mackenzie's frustration peaked again, "JD, I'm sorry, but that doesn't make any sense. You have to go slow to go fast? How does that work?"

JD answered, "When you first start anything new, you have to go into base training mode first. If you push too hard, too fast, you'll totally exhaust yourself, and you end up going slower or will get dropped. Remember that first cycling ride? You pushed so hard, by yourself, for the first fifteen minutes that you had lactic acid build up quickly in your legs. The harder you tried, the slower you went, and your physical pain caused you to quit mentally."

"That's exactly how I feel in my job right now," Mackenzie admitted.

JD nodded. "In cycling you have to put in the miles, starting slow until you have built a solid aerobic base, then you add mileage or speed work. In sales, you have to put in the time to research which contacts are your target suspects, and you have to understand why they are suspects. You do this in order to build your general access base. After you've developed your aerobic base or your general access base, then you can start pushing yourself, in intervals, outside your comfort zone. In cycling you add mileage and speed work; in sales, you work in new techniques over time to move from general access to favorable access. Professionals know this. Amateurs just keep repeating the same training rides over and over and expecting a different result.

"In sales, you have to put in the effort and work your plan to develop your base, your general access. Like I told you on your first ride, 'Keep your eyes looking forward. Align with the wheel in front of you. And do not go to the front of the group.' For you, that means: keep your eyes focused on what you have in front of you, not on what you don't have. Your first goal should be to study those who ride ahead of you and figure out who to align with and how to increase your general access of prospective clients. Second, consider how you can best create favorable access. Don't try to get to the front without building your base first. Go slow now to go fast later."

That made sense to Mackenzie. She had tried to go too fast on her first ride, expecting that she could keep up. She did the same thing with her sales job; she bulldozed through so many cold calls expecting that the sales would automatically happen if she worked hard enough and made the most calls.

JD continued explaining, "You will move up eventually, but you need to hold your position right now and wait for the right timing. In your current position, you have the advantage of riding along, watching, and listening to how the group behaves and works together. Make small moves to position yourself in order to listen and watch from different perspectives. Look for how the leaders in the group push themselves into position to take on new roles. Watch how they add value to the group and thereby pull for the group. This is important. Think about how their pull *for* the group translates to their demand-pull of themselves and, more importantly, increases the efficiency and speed of the group as a whole."

JD looked in her eyes to make sure she was still paying attention and transitioned, "Now, a question for you: in your current position at work, where could you make a small move to increase your own demand-pull in the group?"

"STEPS" OF THE SALES PROCESS

Step 1: Understand your general access.
Step 2: Develop a plan to gain favorable access.

"RULES" OF THE PACELINE

Rule 2: Go slow to go fast.

BOUNCES AND DEPOSITS
Chapter 15

Mackenzie stopped herself from uttering her next answer. Instead, she looked at her palms, thinking, *where could I make a small move at work to increase my own demand-pull?* Her mind was empty. She shook her head and admitted, "I don't know, but I think that you may have an idea?"

JD laughed, "Ha! Now you're learning something. In school, you were graded for knowing the answers. In life, you are graded for understanding the question. Rule 3 is this: Questions are rarely questions. Understand the why."

> **RULE 3**: *Questions are rarely questions.*
> *Understand the why.*

Mackenzie clicked on her phone's notes application and started typing, making a mental note that JD still hadn't introduced Rule 1.

JD continued, "Rule 3 means that you must stop yourself from answering the question; instead, you ask a question to uncover why the question being asked. If you can stop trying to be the one with all the answers, or even stop yourself from talking, you can begin to discover what the other person thinks, feels, and believes. This will lead you to understand what he or she really wants and how you can bring value."

JD let that sink in and continued, "Rule 3 requires Rule 2. You have to go slow and practice hard because we have to change a bad habit in order to move forward. The bad habit we've developed is that we've been trained to know the answers, or at least act like we know them. Rule 3 requires you to stop talking and really listen."

Mackenzie knew she needed to work on this. She had prided herself for knowing the answers before others; she liked to be right and to let others know she was right.

JD kept going, "Then, Rule 3 leads into Rule 4. To illustrate that, tell me: why was Bill denied the $600 loan on his first call to the bank?"

"Because the bank didn't trust he could pay it back," Mackenzie responded confidently, without hesitation.

"Why did you answer the question?" JD asked.

"Because you asked me the question," Mackenzie retorted.

"What's rule 3?" JD asked.

Mackenzie began, "Questions are…"

JD interrupted, "You're answering the question again. Do you think I know the answer?"

"Yes," Mackenzie murmured.

"Since I know the answer, why am I asking the question?" JD challenged.

"Because you want to know that I'm listening?" Mackenzie offered.

"Why did you answer that?" JD chided.

"Because you asked me to?" Mackenzie returned.

"That's the difference between an amateur and a professional salesperson," JD began. "The amateur will answer the question.

The professional will find out why the question is being asked before answering."

Mackenzie was flustered. JD continued, "When someone asks you a question, you have to switch gears and figure out why he is asking the question. What's the easiest way to find out why he is asking?"

"To ask him 'Why?'" Mackenzie attempted.

"Why did you just answer my question?" JD questioned.

"Ugh. I'm so confused. I don't know," Mackenzie answered as her shoulders slumped forward.

JD responded, "First, we are going to have to unteach you what they taught you in school. In school they want you to regurgitate the answer. In business and in life, you need to understand the question. That is the key to understanding what people want. When my wife asks me, 'Would you like to go out to eat tonight?' I answer, 'That's a great idea, what are you thinking about?'

"By answering this way, I positively affirm her idea and my wife tells me why she asked the question in the first place. She has a place in mind, or she has something else on her mind. Either way, I'll find out what she wants and maybe even why she wants something. This technique is called a bounce."

JD paused, then asked, "Mackenzie, how are you feeling right now?"

"Truthfully, I'm overwhelmed," she sighed.

"You just answered my question again," JD frowned. "In school, you've been measured and monitored for knowing the answers. College professors have lectured on 'how to market and advertise' and have forgotten to ask the question of why. Why is it important to market and advertise?"

Mackenzie remained silent, waiting for JD to continue.

"Marketing's job is to help pull the customer to the sale. The purpose of marketing is to first create favorable access for the product, the company, and the salesperson. After favorable access is established, marketing's second phase is to create demand-pull for the product, the company, and the salesperson."

JD paused to pivot to his next point, "To understand how people around us make the decisions that they do, we have to start practicing how to ask the 'why' questions and not just answer their questions with whatever is on our mind. To ask the 'why' questions, we have to have enough trust built up so that others can feel secure in answering those questions candidly. More on that later. Let's get back to the question at hand. Tell me, why was Bill denied the $600 loan on his first call?"

Mackenzie's shoulders tensed as she figured out how to bounce the question. She felt ignorant not answering the question. She was sure she could figure out the answer, but she answered humbly, "JD, that is an interesting question. Why do you think he was denied the $600 loan on his first call?"

"I'm so glad you asked, Mackenzie," JD smiled, knowingly. "You see, I have more background information to the story that you likely did not hear. Bill did not have favorable access with the first banker. The first banker didn't know Bill in a favorable way. He knew that Bill's store was robbed and he was in debt. Bill didn't even try to make conversation with the first banker; he went straight for the take. No one likes to be taken. We often need a reason to trust in order to give."

JD continued, "Bill intuitively asked to be transferred to a person who knew him. For him, it was a last ditch effort, but seeing it from a different perspective, he positioned himself within his favorable access. Bill's direct favorable access with Crawford was relatively weak, as they were mainly acquaintances with a few shared experiences. However, what most people don't know is that what helped strengthen the favorable access was indirectly given, through Bill's wife, Sue. Sue had been a loyal friend to Crawford's wife, Corinne, in college; they had strong favorable access with each other. By association, Bill was given credit due to Sue's favorable investments in her relationships. Bill had credit with Crawford due to Sue's relational investments and his strong connection to Sue as her husband. Sue made relational deposits into people, which benefited her husband. So, whether the relational deposits are made directly or indirectly, favorable access is increased."

Mackenzie nodded. By bouncing the question, it gave JD the opportunity to tell more of the story and connect more dots. If she had attempted to answer with her limited knowledge, JD might not have shared his insight.

JD continued, "Personal and business relationships are, in the simplest sense, like banking relationships. When you want to increase your relational worth in a friendship, you give something of value. When you want to increase your financial worth in a banking relationship, you deposit. If you try to take before you have any worth built up, you will have a hard time being successful in sales and in relationships.

"Which brings us to Rule 4: Make significant deposits before withdrawing or asking for a loan."

RULE 4: *Make significant deposits before withdrawing or asking for a loan.*

JD allowed her to type out the rule before he continued. "When you withdraw something, you take it. When you ask for a loan, you are asking to be granted the temporary use of something, and you will pay back an extra percentage to use it. Making a deposit, on the other hand, is giving something of value to someone you trust will hold onto it."

JD paused again. "As I said earlier, we often need a reason to trust in order to give. So you, as a young and unestablished salesperson, have to be the one who initiates giving, making deposits, in order to establish trust. When you have earned the trust, you make it easier for someone else to invite you towards favorable access." JD paused again and waited.

"But what do I give? What kind of deposits do I need to make?" Mackenzie asked.

"Great questions. That depends on how well you've practiced Rules 2 and 3. You'll have to do your homework and ask the right questions, and keep asking, to figure out what will bring value. This takes hard work, patience, and time."

JD's answer frustrated Mackenzie. Another puzzle. She just wanted a concrete starting point, a cornerstone piece, and she felt like he was giving her random middle pieces to a puzzle with one thousand pieces. She attempted a question that would bring out more information from JD, like a bounce. "JD, from your vast experience, have you discovered any conversational themes that bring value?" She felt like she was pandering, but she needed something, anything, to grasp onto.

"Mackenzie, you're practicing, and I appreciate that. When you are working with your general access group, in a casual setting, this is where you start with small talk. So, I'll give you three basic themes on where to deposit: their health, their wealth, and their relationships. These three topics can be tricky because people have a lot of emotion wrapped up in them. Tread lightly at first and take notes. When you know enough to bring value to one of these three, then you'll be able to build trust enough to ask better questions to find what else your prospect values."

Mackenzie felt relieved to have a starting point.

JD continued, "You'll need to practice Rules 2, 3, and 4 in order to make it more natural for you and your prospects. Otherwise, your words will sound cheap and self-serving. So, practice by making verbal deposits of kindness into total strangers and observe how your words can affect people you don't even know. Then graduate to acts of kindness, lending a helping hand in a practical way, and observe how the other person's behavior toward you changes. Make those same deposits into family and friends and observe how it strengthens your connections. When you practice these Rules of the Paceline enough to turn your actions into habits, then you'll start making deposits not to expect something in return, but to practice how to be a person who values others first."

JD leaned forward, "But when you are with a prospect at a business meeting, remember that you need to focus on your prospect's work problems. That is not a time for chit-chat. That is a time to make their work easier by helping them find a solution to their work problems. That is where we start using The Steps." JD glanced at his watch and said, "Which we can go into more detail later. So, now can you answer the question you started this conversation with, Mackenzie?"

With all of this new information, Mackenzie had forgotten what she had asked. JD stepped in, "You asked, 'How do I position myself to achieve favorable access and create demand-pull for the product I'm trying to sell?' Using what you learned, how would you answer your question now?"

Mackenzie was amazed at his recall. Before she answered, she stopped herself and replied, "JD that is such a great question. I know you'll have the best answer."

JD laughed. "Now I'm actually asking you a question to understand what you learned from what I taught you. Go ahead."

"Okay. Hmmm. Well, using Rule 3, I asked my question for a reason. I wanted you to help me. Truthfully," Mackenzie hesitated, "I think I was trying to get to the end-result without putting in the work. I wanted a quick fix. I wanted you to tell me how to get a sale. You instead told me about the work I need to do before I can make a sale."

"Yep. Go on," JD encouraged.

"Okay, so I also think I used the terms in the wrong order.

From what you taught me, if my product or service doesn't yet have demand-pull, I need to develop demand-pull. But it's not by showing someone how great I am; it's about being a person that brings value to someone else's problem. So, I need to position myself to practice Rules 3 and 4 with and for others." Mackenzie paused, and an idea popped into her head. "Basically, you're having me practice how to pull for others, right?"

JD nodded.

"Okay, that makes sense. When I create a pull for others, I become someone who others want to follow. When I pull for others and bring a solution to their perceived problem, I create a demand, something they need or have to have." Mackenzie's thoughts clicked together, and then she thought out loud, "Shouldn't it be called pull-demand?"

JD chuckled. "Well, you can call it whatever you want. Once you start working on this, you'll realize that it's a continuous process, not a once-and-done action. It's pull-demand; demand-pull. Just like pedaling your bike, push-pull, pull-push, you have to build enough demand to earn the right to stay up front, then you voluntarily cycle through and encourage the team. And you don't quit there; you're just getting started. After you've practiced this for years, you'll understand how to create demand first, and you'll reinforce the demand by pulling for others and them, in turn, pulling for you. The group will then start to respect and appreciate your abilities. But, don't forget why you are working on your pull and creating demand. Why are you doing all of this work?"

"For favorable access," Mackenzie quickly stated.

"That's pretty selfish and shallow, don't you think? What's the underlying reason?"

Instead of kicking herself for the wrong answer, she paused and smiled, thinking of a bounce and finally enjoying this puzzle, "There's a deeper question. I don't think my answer will be as good as yours. I'd love to know your answer to that, JD."

"Why, Mackenzie, I'm flattered," JD grinned. "You are doing all of this work to build trust. When you build solid trust, when someone else knows they can depend on you, you receive an invitation to the front."

Just like Lisa did for me. Because she had seen what I could do on the spin bike, she trusted that I would be an asset to the paceline and invited me to join the team. "Right. Of course. Sorry, I get so focused on the end result, I forget the bigger picture. And when I see the bigger picture, I sometimes forget where I started…which actually brings me back to the reason for my question. Where do I start?"

"You start where you are," JD answered. "You start with your current position, with your new perspective. Instead of looking out for yourself, you're looking beyond yourself. You actively look for situations where you can practice Rules 2, 3, and 4."

JD continued, "Positioning yourself to listen and learn and apply what you learn at your job should be a daily practice. It will lead you to understand yourself and those around you, which will help you understand why Rule number one is Rule 1."

Mackenzie took the bait, "And what is Rule 1?"

JD replied, "When you have made a habit out of wanting to give without thinking about your gain, then you will be ready to know about the number 1 Rule."

Mackenzie typed more notes on her phone and JD stated, "Mackenzie, you can do this. I'll see you on Thursday's ride. Make it a great day."

"STEPS" OF THE SALES PROCESS

Step 1: Understand your general access.
Step 2: Develop a plan to gain favorable access.

"RULES" OF THE PACELINE

Rule 2: Go slow to go fast.
Rule 3: Questions are rarely questions. Understand the why.
Rule 4: Make significant deposits before withdrawing or asking for a loan.

START WHERE YOU ARE
Chapter 16

As Mackenzie stepped into the elevator at work, her mind was flooded with JD's lessons. Two of her co-workers, Jack and Tommy, ran in right behind her. Jack looked and acted like a bulldog; he was thick set, with broad shoulders and would persistently and aggressively chase deals. He was the only one of the new-hire salespeople who had closed a handful of deals in their first three months. Tommy, on the other hand, was a former college football kicker, who was good under pressure but struggled with how to call his own shots. He was used to being told what to do on the field and wasn't sure how to run his own game. He had been following Stan's sales strategies and had yet to kick one through the goalposts.

"Ah, man, even running to the elevator hurts. I've got to go get this checked out. Hey, do either of you know a good dentist?" Tommy asked, looking to his two co-workers.

Jack was quick to answer, "Sorry man, that sucks. I hate dentists. I don't trust dentists just like I don't trust mechanics. I take my car in for a $40 oil change and next thing you know, they're telling me that my brake and steering fluids need to be flushed, my alignment is off, and my timing belt is about to fail. I know my car well enough to know they're full of it. And my teeth are fine too. Last time I went to the dentist was 3 years ago, and he told me I was in the beginning stages of gingivitis and periodontal disease. He said it like I was dying. And wouldn't you know it, after I went to that dentist, my teeth hurt for two weeks! I don't trust anyone who uses fear to make me do what they recommend. And I am not going back to any dentist until my teeth start falling out."

All three of them laughed at the truth of his story. It felt good to laugh together about something they all had in common. It was easy to bond over bashing a common enemy.

Then JD's words echoed in her mind, "Start where you are."

Jack sprinted off to his cubicle, and Mackenzie turned to Tommy and asked, "What kind of tooth pain are you having, Tommy?" She didn't know much about teeth, but she could relate to pain. His tooth pain was severe, but he hadn't been to a dentist in a few years, just like Mackenzie and Jack.

The conversation that followed unearthed more than tooth pain, revealing his complaints at work, being new to the city, and frustrated that the sales job wasn't going according to the plan Stan had sold him on. Mackenzie was present with JD's wisdom fueling her concern, questions, and listening. In the middle of another of Tommy's responses, a memory from the morning's ride popped into her head. As she listened to the chatter during the recovery section of the ride, she had overheard Lisa recommending her dentist with high regard.

Mackenzie continued to listen to Tommy's complaints and said, "Come to think of it, I may have a dentist to recommend. Let me ask around and I'll get back to you by tomorrow."

Tommy's face changed from pain to appreciation. "Oh, Mackenzie, that would be awesome. All of the reviews online that I've checked out have been mixed bags. I've been putting in so many hours here at work, and I just don't have time to mess around checking out a bunch of dentists, who I don't trust in the first place."

As Mackenzie walked to her desk, she thought she'd go ahead and make an appointment for herself. If she was going to recommend someone, then she'd feel better by knowing first hand. She called Lisa, got the name of the dentist, and then called the dentist's office. Due to an earlier cancellation, they had an opening for her to have an initial visit a few hours later. After the receptionist took down her pertinent information, she was set for her appointment. Mackenzie thought to herself, *I wish my sales could happen that fast.*

A SYSTEMATIC APPROACH
Chapter 17

Mackenzie's dental hygienist was friendly and thorough. While the office was sparsely decorated, they had invested in a few key technologies including digital screens and headsets that allowed her to watch a few pre-selected entertaining video casts while she was getting her teeth cleaned. She learned some interesting tidbits in the video casts and was thankful that she didn't have to answer mundane questions while a hygienist shoved a fistful of sharp instruments in her mouth.

Dr. Evan placed himself in the hygienist's chair once she was finished. "Mackenzie, I'm grateful that Lisa recommended me to you. She and the entire cycling group have been instrumental in my practice. If I had known how many cyclists were looking for a new dentist, I would have introduced myself to the group months ago! I guess we all need someone to look out for us."

Dr. Evan asked a few questions about her hygiene habits and gave her a few recommendations, ending with, "We'll send you a reminder to keep those pearly-whites healthy. Do you have any questions for me?"

"Actually, Dr. Evan, I do have a few." Mackenzie found out

that, yes, he had joined the cycling group a few years ago. Then she told him about her co-worker Tommy and said, "You seem like someone I can trust to be honest. Are you the doctor to perform difficult dental procedures?"

Dr. Evan responded, "Mackenzie, I believe I'm the best oral surgeon in the state. But, we've all heard that before. I don't want you to just take my word for it. Hmmm, yes. At this Thursday's ride, I'll introduce you to Ted Whitman, and I'll have him tell you about his experience with his procedure. You can ask him how he's feeling now."

That name sounded familiar to Mackenzie. "That would be great, Dr. Evan. I'll see you at tomorrow's ride. Thanks!" After a few more pleasantries, Mackenzie walked out of the dental office.

Ted Whitman. Whitman, she repeated to herself. She had called on a company named Whitman Distributing at least twenty times and had left the CEO and HR Director several voicemails but never received a returned call. She pulled out her phone and looked up Whitman Distributing's 'About Us' section of their website. Whitman's owner and CEO was Ted Whitman. *Well, how lucky is that?* And then she remembered what JD said, "What looks like luck to the untrained eye, is really a systematic approach to the sales process."

DEPOSIT FIRST
Chapter 18

Mackenzie arrived early to the ride, on the lookout for Dr. Evan. He arrived a few minutes later, saw Mackenzie, and waved her over. Mackenzie had rehearsed a few questions that she thought to ask Dr. Evan before meeting Ted Whitman.

"Good morning, Dr. Evan! Is Mr. Whitman planning to ride this morning?" She meant to ask that question later, but her nervousness made her jump in too early. She reminded herself to take it slow, despite knowing her sales goal timeline was drawing near. She scolded herself, *this isn't about you, right now, Mackenzie! This is about finding information for Tommy. That's it. Deposit first. Build trust. Loans come later.*

"I did connect with Ted yesterday and said he'd be here a few minutes early to talk with you. How are you doing this morning?" Dr. Evan replied.

"Great! That's really nice of Mr. Whitman to be a referral for you. So how long have you known Mr. Whitman?" Mackenzie hoped she wasn't prying too much with her questions, but she knew she needed to find out more about Ted Whitman.

"Ted was a patient at the practice where I formerly worked.

He was my colleague's patient. Ted and I didn't know each other well but recognized each other once I started cycling with this group. After I left the group practice to start my own, Ted had a root canal procedure. My former colleague performed the surgery, and it failed. Ted was in so much pain that he had me take a look to see if there were anything I could do to help him. He was in bad shape. But that's why I love being a dentist; I like to restore order and confidence. With Ted, I happened to be at the right place at the right time to lessen his pain and fix what was wrong. Ted is a stand-up guy and didn't sue my colleague, and I'll tell you what; Ted is my best advertisement. He is an extremely busy man with his work, but he's more than willing to tell anyone how I saved him from his pain. That's just the kind of guy he is. I just did my job and did it well."

"Wow, sounds like you really made a difference for Mr. Whitman." Mackenzie wanted to grill Dr. Evan about Ted's interests outside of cycling, his family, whatever she could find, but she decided to focus on Dr. Evan. "Dr. Evan, how has it been running your own practice? I have some friends who started their own businesses. It seems like there are a lot of moving parts."

"Oh, there are a lot of moving parts, all right. Thankfully, I have worked long enough in the industry to bring people on my team who I know are great at what they do. Client acquisition was really difficult in the beginning, though. We're dentists, not salespeople. I thought it was a bit hokey to introduce myself to the cycling group, but a mentor I really respect encouraged me to do it. I never would have thought it would generate as much new traffic as it has, but JD knew it would, and I trust his business instincts. Oh, hey, look there's Ted." Dr. Evan waved at Ted, and he walked over to them.

Mackenzie's mind was racing. *JD mentored Dr. Evan too? What is he, like the Batman of business?* She mused. *A man dressed up like a biker, who fights against mediocrity in sales and mentors the next genera-*

tion to the next level. Yep. I think that about sums it up. How does he do it all? She silently questioned. But she didn't have time to question more because Ted was walking their way.

"Ted, I'd like to introduce you to Mackenzie Jones. Before she recommends me to her co-worker for a difficult dental procedure, she asked me to rate myself as a technical oral surgeon." Dr. Evan grinned, "I thought it would be better hearing it from the mouth of someone who I've worked on."

"Hello there, Mackenzie. Smart woman, you are. Lots of people will lie to your face. Always ask for a referral. Your name sounds familiar, but I can't quite pinpoint it."

Mackenzie stopped herself from interjecting that she had left him and the HR Director several voicemails each. *Deposit first, Mackenzie.* Instead, she just smiled and said, "It's a common name. So, Dr. Evan has told me how you've been instrumental to his practice. That is really kind of you."

"I wouldn't call it kind. He saved me from my pain. Mackenzie, have you ever had a nerve next to your brain that caused blinding headaches? I couldn't think, I couldn't eat, I couldn't sleep. My dentist told me the pain would go away in a few weeks. I expect integrity and results from people I do business with, and that includes dentists. No excuses. On week three, I was mad. So mad that I caused two new work hires to quit in one day. That evening, my wife told me to stop blaming her for my pain and go ride my bike. I got up the next morning, still in pain, and rode my bike to get my mind off my misery." Ted pointed to Dr. Evan, "This guy rode behind me, drafting me until I hit a wall. Then I rode his wheel for a while. He asked me how I was doing. I cursed my dentist. Evan told me he was a dentist. I cursed him and all dentists that he was related to. I told him that dentists don't deserve the title 'Doctor.'"

Ted turned to Dr. Evan, and they both laughed. Ted continued, "Evan told me he'd clear his schedule that morning and see me immediately. He fixed my tooth that day and arranged for someone to drive me home. Now, *that* is getting things done and done right. No excuses. You tell your co-worker to get his face in to see Dr. Evan immediately."

"Yes, sir," Mackenzie replied. And she meant it. Mackenzie didn't know what else to say other than, "Will do. Thank you, Mr. Whitman."

"You're welcome," Ted nodded.

Mackenzie knew she would not get many opportunities with Mr. Ted Whitman. Despite being intimidated, she knew she had to capitalize on this meeting. She tried to think of one of the questions she had prepared to segue into her work, but none of them seemed to fit. After fulfilling his duty, Ted looked to Dr. Evan and nodded, as if to signal his departure. Mackenzie quickly asked, "Mr. Whitman, when you were no longer in pain, did you ask those two employees to return?"

"What? Which employees? Oh, yeah, I did mention that, didn't I? Ha! Definitely not. I just accelerated the inevitable. HR wasn't happy with me. My HR Director said we had already invested so much into their training, but I figure that it gives her a chance to hire better next time. Young people today are too soft. Your generation wants a ribbon for showing up to work. There are no participation medals in the real world."

This comment didn't surprise Mackenzie; she had been told this about her generation before so she didn't take the comment personally. "I have heard great things about your company, Mr. Whitman. You really found a niche market and continue to serve them well."

Ted Whitman turned his chin to the side and said, "What have you heard about my company, Mackenzie?" Dr. Evan's posture changed as well. Clearly, her comments and interest in Mr. Whitman's business were unexpected.

Mackenzie was a bit shocked that she was given the floor, "The history of your company is truly impressive, Mr. Whitman. You sought out distribution rights with local manufacturers when most distributors were looking to partner with overseas manufacturers..." as she talked, she thought about the steps, *Am I already in favorable access? Do I need to slow down? Have I made enough deposits? Questions are rarely questions. Ack! Bounce this, Mackenzie!*

Mackenzie stopped herself, "But you already know all of this. What makes you ask that, Mr. Whitman?"

"We spend a lot of money on marketing and advertising and no one seems to know what we do. That and it's hard to find good talent. If you'd like a job at Whitman Distributing, call up my HR Director. We need young people like you working for us, who actually care about something other than themselves. I don't understand your generation, but you give me a little hope for the future."

Mackenzie and Dr. Evan laughed, and Mr. Whitman made his exit. Dr. Evan turned to Mackenzie and said, "I'm not sure what you do, but I think you just made a really good impression."

Mackenzie returned, "Thank you, Dr. Evan. You mentioned that you know JD. He's taught me a lot in the past week."

"You know JD too? He's the one who encouraged me to start my own practice and totally changed my mindset with clients and how I do business. He and his wife are amazing. I hope to return the favor someday."

NEXT STEP

Chapter 19

After the morning ride, she saw Luke's text to her, "I'm running late, but I'm going to make it to the Dynamo this morning. Let's grab coffee afterwards."

She was happy to see that Luke reached out, but his timing was off. She didn't have time for coffee with Luke. She had to find JD for him to tell her the next Steps & Rules in order to know how to proceed with Mr. Whitman.

Finally, she spotted him. JD was talking with a muscular young man with tousled hair who appeared to be taking notes. *How many people does he mentor? And that other guy has calves like Wes, except maybe better.*

She angled her walking path so that she could see the mystery man's face and stopped abruptly. The muscular young man talking to JD was Luke. Her mouth dropped open with surprise.

JD and Luke turned to her. Luke exclaimed, "Mackenzie! Thanks for finding me."

JD paused and said, "You two know each other?"

Mackenzie, flustered by her attraction to Luke, suddenly became serious so as to make sure Luke didn't notice the heat rising to her face, "Yes, we do. Hi, Luke. JD, I'm sorry to interrupt. May I ask you a question after you two finish talking?"

"What does it have to do with?" JD asked.

"Where should I go after favorable access?" Mackenzie questioned.

"Well, this will benefit both of you," JD looked to Luke and Mackenzie, "so ask it now."

"Really?" Mackenzie responded, wondering why Luke was learning a sales process. "Okay," she said, "so I just met the CEO of one of the companies where I want to sell my product. What is the next step after favorable access?"

"Tell me the first two steps," JD instructed.

"Step 1: Understand your general access. Then, Step 2: Develop a plan to gain favorable access," Mackenzie recited.

"Correct," JD stared at Mackenzie.

Mackenzie knew he was insinuating that she was still at Step 2: Develop a plan to gain favorable access. But, she didn't have time to stay at Step 2; she needed to know what to do after Step 2 so that she could move faster. "Okay," she admitted her agreement, "So let's say I continue to deposit and move toward favorable access. Then what is Step 3?"

JD had witnessed this scene too many times to count, and he knew that she would have to learn the hard way with her own experience. He answered, "Step 3 is: Leverage favorable access to get a meeting."

STEP 3: *Leverage favorable access to get a meeting.*

Mackenzie nodded, "So would I ask for a meeting with him?"

"Again, remember Rule 2, you have to go slow to go fast," JD reminded her. "Stop and ask yourself a few questions. Is the

CEO the person who will make the decision on buying your product?"

"I would think he would have the final say," Mackenzie responded.

"Is the CEO going to be the one to implement your product?" JD asked.

"No," Mackenzie admitted.

"Who at the company will implement and who will use your product?" JD asked again and then continued, "Depending on the introduction and the impression, your weak favorable access may be enough for him to open the door to someone else at the company. Your move from general access to favorable access with someone at the top reverts back to general access when you are introduced to someone within his circle. It's best to establish strong favorable access before asking for a referral. Once you do that, research who you need an introduction to, and do all of the legwork. Do not make the CEO do any more work than to forward a message or something just as simple."

"Thank you, JD," she replied. Although she still wasn't sure what she was supposed to do next, she waved goodbye to both JD and Luke and got on her bike to speed home then get to work. She'd have coffee with Luke another day.

On the way home, she tried to focus on what she would do as a next step instead of thinking about Luke but her mind kept drifting back to him. *Why is JD teaching Luke the Steps & Rules? Luke is a computer programmer – he's not in sales! Why does Luke care about a sales process?*

"STEPS" OF THE SALES PROCESS

Step 1: Understand your general access.
Step 2: Develop a plan to gain favorable access.
Step 3: Leverage favorable access to get a meeting.

"RULES" OF THE PACELINE

Rule 2: Go slow to go fast.
Rule 3: Questions are rarely questions. Understand the why.
Rule 4: Make significant deposits before withdrawing or asking for a loan.

EXTRA MILE
Chapter 20

When Mackenzie returned to work that morning, she ran up to Tommy and excitedly shared, "I found your dentist! I talked with someone who had a botched root canal, and Dr. Evan fixed him. He's your guy. Here's the number. He's expecting your call."

"I can't call now; I've got to get my Sales Excellence metrics entered before the meeting. I'll call after the meeting," Tommy answered.

"You're the one dealing with the pain. One call and that pain will go away," Mackenzie responded with a too-bright smile on her face.

Tommy furrowed his brow. "So, what's in it for you? Do you get some referral bonus or something?" Tommy winced as he put his hand to his cheek to ease the pain.

Mackenzie was irritated by his question, "No, I don't get a referral bonus. Seriously, Tommy?" She felt her annoyance rising, "I took time out of my day to check out the practice. Then the dentist went out of his way to introduce me to someone who he had just worked on so that I'd feel comfortable referring you to him. I wanted to make sure he was a good dentist. Sorry for going the extra mile for you," Mackenzie huffed.

"Okay! You're right. I'll call. Thanks, Mackenzie."

"You're welcome," Mackenzie stomped off. She did want to make a deposit towards Dr. Evan to increase her favorable access with him and his network, so in a way, her deposit could end up being a referral bonus. But she didn't want to tell Tommy that. She felt a little uncomfortable with the tension of wanting Tommy to follow through not just to alleviate his pain, but also for her own benefit of favorable access. JD had told her, "Make deposits not to expect something in return, but to practice how to be a person who values others first." It was not her initial plan to get something in return for the dentist recommendation, but that happened to be a by-product.

Tommy should at least be grateful for all the work I've done for him! Whatever. I've got work to do. She set off to understand who at Whitman Distributing would be a good decision maker and how to ask for an introduction.

HITTING SEND

Chapter 21

Mackenzie reviewed the "Sales Manual" document that the sales crew was given on their first training day. "Welcome to OnBoardMobile.com! Our product is an employee on-boarding system, delivered via mobile device..." and she skimmed to, "Sales Connection: The CEO, CFO, and HR Director are the ideal contacts..."

Mackenzie talked quietly to herself trying to organize her thoughts, "Mr. Whitman already told me to contact his HR Director. He is a no-nonsense, do-not-cross, no-mercy type of guy. But he's also willing to help others who earn his respect. Okay, so I got introduced to the CEO by making a deposit for a coworker, which was also a deposit for the dentist. The dentist had favorable access with Mr. Whitman and is using his favorable access to further his business with this referral.

"Do I have strong enough access now with Mr. Whitman to ask for a referral? Probably not. But I don't have time to build strong favorable access. So, maybe I could make a deposit for the HR Director. What kind of deposit?"

Mackenzie answered her own question, "I have no idea. Do I

always need to make a deposit? Maybe JD is wrong, and my general access is really favorable access. Therefore, Mr. Whitman should be able to introduce me. Maybe I should just be bold and go for it. I bet Mr. Whitman will appreciate my follow-up and will open the door to HR for me."

After wrestling with several options, Mackenzie decided to write an email to Mr. Whitman. After all, JD had mentioned, 'Don't make the CEO do anything more than forward an email.' She figured that this was the most efficient use of her time and probably Mr. Whitman's time as well.

From: MJones@onboardmobile.com
Date: Thursday, 10:45 AM
To: TWhitman@WhitmanDistributing.com
Subject: Following up

Dear Mr. Whitman,
It was an honor meeting you this morning. You mentioned that I should contact your HR Director, Karen Smith, if I would like a job at Whitman Distributing. I truly appreciate your advice. I am committed to my current work, and through my work, I believe I can serve Mrs. Smith and your company in a different way.

Will you please forward this email to Karen?

Respectfully,
Mackenzie Jones
Mobile Employee On-boarding
Your Company Vision, Multiplied

Mackenzie felt affirmed that she had made the right choice in efficiency when only a few minutes later she saw that Mr. Whitman had forwarded her email to Karen and cc'd her on it. She opened the email, expecting an introduction from Mr. Whitman. There was no introduction, just a forwarded email. "Not exactly what I was looking for, but I can work with this," Mackenzie muttered to herself. She drafted her reply.

From: MJones@onboardmobile.com
Date: Thursday, 10:55 AM
To: KSmith@WhitmanDistributing.com
Subject: Re: FW: Following up

Mrs. Smith,

As an HR Director of a great company like Whitman Distributing, you are responsible for recruiting, hiring, on-boarding, benefits, morale, and the list goes on. As Mr. Whitman expressed, my millennial generation is difficult to keep engaged and on-task with the responsibilities of efficiency and excellence. If I may have ten minutes of your time, I would like to ask you about your current systems and how I may be able to serve you.

I will follow up this email with a phone call to you.

Sincerely,
Mackenzie Jones
Mobile Employee On-boarding
Your Company Vision, Multiplied

Mackenzie hit send. And waited. And waited. Then her computer alerted her of the sales team meeting, and her phone reminder buzzed for a meeting with Bill Reichardt. She grabbed the company car keys and ran.

SHIFTING PERSPECTIVE
Chapter 22

As Mackenzie sat down in the chair across from Bill and brought the small talk to a close, she started in with what was on her mind. "Bill, you used your favorable access from being a football star. Your wife had an impressive social network which granted you a larger circle of favorable access. I don't have any of that. I don't come from an important family; I grew up with my mom working two and sometimes three part-time jobs. My dad left when I was a toddler. I'm not starting with much of a foundation to build favorable access, and I can't figure out what value I can add to these important business men's lives."

"Stories are interesting, aren't they?" Bill asked. "You hear what you want to hear so that you can either use it to motivate you or blame something or someone when things don't go your way. It's all about your perspective. We all fight silent battles in our minds. It's your thoughts about what happens that will determine your path forward."

Bill paused, then began, "When I was born, my parents managed a small diner called Reich's Café. It was open twenty-four hours a day, every day. My parents worked there around the clock. My grandmother took care of me until I was six. The Café was the only place I could get a warm meal, but if my parents saw me, they'd make me work. I learned to eat really fast so I could get my backside outta there. I didn't want to wait tables because the customers would complain about everything. 'My fries are cold. The service is too slow. This burger isn't cooked the way I want it.' This was a café, not a fine-dining establishment! They paid pennies but expected a five-star meal.

"I was a kid who didn't like being yelled at for something I couldn't do anything about. So my mom told me if I didn't want to wait tables, I'd have to peel potatoes. In the basement. I was alone in the basement and I hated being alone, but it was better than dealing with complaining customers who didn't leave a tip. And I could sneak out of the grate in the basement. Then, I'd go stand on the street corner, just to talk to people so I didn't feel alone. I talked to anyone and everyone.

"When I started playing football at Iowa, people took notice that I was always talking. I was always challenging everyone on the field and had such a loud mouth that they called me Noise Box. Noise Box and Bill the Bull." Bill laughed again.

"Good thing I wasn't talking when I first saw Sue," Bill joked. "She was up on a stage, being crowned the Iowa Interfraternity Queen. I fell in love at first sight. She was beautiful. I asked my friends about her. She was smart. She was sweet. But she was from a family that lived a big life of luxury. Her father had owned a Chrysler dealership in Des Moines. She and her family lived the lives of socialites. Sue was a lady. I barely used a fork when I ate my meals. She was way out of my league." Bill smirked.

Mackenzie was intrigued and ventured, "So how'd you catch such a lady?"

Bill lost himself in thought for a moment. Mackenzie had read about Sue dying from Alzheimer's five years prior, and imagined that Bill was reflecting on her life. "Well, on the surface, Sue had it all. But, when you stop to listen, you'll realize that everyone has a need. Sue's dad died during her sophomore year of college. She was a daddy's girl. His death rocked her precious world.

"Looking back, if she hadn't lost her father two years prior, I never would have stood a chance getting a date with Sue." Bill looked up for a brief moment. Then, just as quickly, a twinkle in his eyes returned. "But at the time I met her, she was looking for a man who was confident and strong. I had just received the Big 10 MVP award, and she was impressed.

"When we started dating seriously, Sue drove me to Des Moines where her mother set up a handful of social engagements." Bill leaned forward, placing five fingers on the desktop, "Now, on the football field, I was never intimidated. I knew I had practiced harder and I could hit harder than any other guy on the field.

"The Des Moines social engagements were a different kind of game with social rules that I didn't understand. These were well-dressed older gentlemen and ladies who talked with finesse. I was a street-kid jock forced into what felt like ballet tryouts in my one and only suit that I had bought after they awarded me the MVP trophy. Sue led the conversations, and when I'd say something, I was ignored or made to feel like my opinion didn't matter. I decided I didn't like those people, I didn't like their game, and I decided that I didn't have to learn to play their game.

"Right after Sue and I were married during the summer of 1952 we moved to Wisconsin for the Green Bay Packers preseason, back on my turf, where I was comfortable. However, after one season, I joined the Air Force at the Bolling Air Force Base in DC. It was better to join than to be drafted to war. I had already lost a lot of friends in the war."

Bill leaned back in his chair, "My time in the Air Force was a maturing season for me. Although I didn't want to obey the Air

Force rules and requirements, these rules were to be followed because our lives depended on it. I was put in my place and told directly that my opinion did not matter. The well-heeled gentleman and ladies from Sue's social engagements in Des Moines were cupcakes in comparison.

"What my Air Force commanding officers taught me would keep me alive on the battlefield. Listen and learn now or die early. I had a vested interest in learning from them, and I trusted them with my life. The Air Force officers carried themselves confidently, they spoke intelligently, and they dressed sharply. I started to take notice of the details.

"This was also the time when Bud opened up our Sports Shop. Sue and I would return to Des Moines eventually, and I decided that it was worth it to learn better ways to carry myself, speak, and dress. I didn't want to fake my manners; I wanted them to become part of who I was becoming. JD's Rule 5 is: Practice until the process becomes instinctive.

RULE 5: *Practice until the process becomes instinctive.*

"Committing yourself to practice until the process becomes instinctive, is what I call excellent practice. In order to commit yourself to excellent practice, you need to decide that it is worth it. You need to understand your reason why you want to change your well-worn habits. No one else can make this decision for you because no one is going to practice for you.

"I decided to commit to excellent practice to improve my first impression with others, to improve my social skills, and learn the dress codes because I wanted to be confident selling to those well-heeled gentlemen back in Des Moines. You have to constantly practice new techniques in order to train yourself before it becomes a new habit, before it becomes instinctive and before you'll experience the full benefits. It is awkward learning new skills as an adult."

As Mackenzie listened to Bill share his decision, she flashbacked to Lisa's advice in spin class. Just like anything worth doing, it would take dedicated time to develop and instill muscle memory so that practice would become not just a habit but an instinct.

"Excellent practice isn't just committing the time and going out there to drill through the same things day after day. Excellent practice is about pushing yourself outside your comfort zone, trying new techniques and often grinding through when you're tired or bored and until you get to the next level. You have to go through the grind to become more refined. As I practiced, I felt more confident in my ability to converse with people from all walks of life."

Bill continued, "I wasn't changing who I was; I was refining myself. I found out that many men were entertained by my football stories. I started to bring something of value to them. Laughter. I learned I was good at making others laugh, making them feel good.

"These men had also lost many friends in the war. They felt valued when I showed interest in who they were and the battles they had already faced. This brings us back to your battle. Your mom was a hard worker and didn't have time to build relationships, other than with you. You grew up without a father. I'm sorry that your father left when you were young. That's a hole only God can fill – if you let him. You make your own decisions, control your thoughts, and determine your own actions.

"Your decisions, thoughts, and actions shape your future responses and become the breaking or the making of who you will be. Just because you weren't given a network of favorable access doesn't mean you can't build one. It will take practice. It will be awkward at first. You'll have to decide to commit to practice until the process becomes instinctive.

"You practice to improve how you meet people, improve your social skills, improve the way to add value to others. You have ways in which you can help anyone, be it a kid on the street or an important businessman. Every relationship can start by simply being an intentional listener while asking a few good, well-timed questions."

Bill winced as he leaned back in his chair again. "So, Mackenzie, are you going to let a bunch of old people intimidate you? Or are you going to practice showing them that you give a damn?"

Mackenzie smiled, feeling motivated with Bill's optimism, "I'm going to practice showing those old people that I give a damn."

"Good," Bill replied. "Because my back is killing me. Can you help me up?"

"STEPS" OF THE SALES PROCESS

Step 1: Understand your general access.
Step 2: Develop a plan to gain favorable access.
Step 3: Leverage favorable access to get a meeting.

"RULES" OF THE PACELINE

Rule 2: Go slow to go fast.
Rule 3: Questions are rarely questions. Understand the why.
Rule 4: Make significant deposits before withdrawing or asking for a loan.
Rule 5: <u>Practice until the process becomes instinctive.</u>

PREPARATION MATTERS
Chapter 23

Mackenzie didn't check her work email until she arrived at her desk the next morning. As she scanned the unread email subjects, one made her heart skip a beat.

From: KSmith@WhitmanDistributing.com
Date: Thursday, 6:41 PM
To: MJones@onboardmobile.com
Subject: Re: FW: Re: Following up

Mackenzie,
I have 10 minutes tomorrow morning to hear about your services. I'll expect you at 9 AM.
-Karen

It was 8:15 AM. The drive would be about 30 minutes with traffic. She regretted her choice of clothing, thinking she would be staying in the office on the casual Friday. She wouldn't have time to go home and change. She rationalized, *It's a distributing company. It'll be fine.* She grabbed her purse, the company car keys, her sales portfolio, and headed for the door.

On her way out, Stan saw Mackenzie, jumped out of his cubicle, and ran-walked after her. "Mackenzie, we need to talk. You missed the sales meeting on Monday and the follow-up meeting yesterday. I still don't see any new pipeline accounts in the system for this week. What is going on?"

"Sorry, Stan. I'll talk with you when I get back. I have a meeting with a prospect right now, and I can't be late."

"Is this prospect on your pipeline?" Stan glared.

"I'll explain later. Sorry, gotta go," Mackenzie waved.

Stan stood there, stunned with a look of distaste spreading across his face.

She was thankful to get out of the door. She had been avoiding Stan all week because she didn't want to talk about numbers when she was learning about building relationships. But she didn't have time to think about it.

She started feeling nervous as she drove to the Whitman headquarters, so she gave herself a pep talk, "Okay, Mackenzie. Remember, this isn't about you. Questions are rarely questions. Bounce her questions and figure out what is underneath her question. Seek to understand. You have favorable access with Mr. Whitman. Well, at least you're close enough to favorable access. Remind Karen that Mr. Whitman told you to contact her. That will help bring you closer to favorable access with her. You've got this, Mackenzie." As she reminded herself of her favorable access, she felt more confident that it would be a great meeting.

She arrived at Whitman Distributing at 8:50 AM. *Perfect.* At the front desk, Mackenzie stated her meeting with Mrs. Smith for 9 AM, then sat down to await her arrival. At 8:59 AM, a middle-aged woman, wearing a black mid-calf skirt, white button-down, and black pumps arrived at the front desk.

Mackenzie, in her wrinkled khaki pants and a sleeveless shirt, kicked herself for not going home to wear a more professional shirt and pressed pants. *Too late now.*

Mrs. Smith glanced quickly at Mackenzie, scanned almost unnoticeably at what Mackenzie was wearing, and extended her hand with a forced smile. "Hello. Mackenzie, I presume?"

"Yes. Mrs. Smith, thank you for meeting me this morning," Mackenzie greeted.

"You're welcome. It's a busy day, so we'll go right to this conference room over here and get right to the point."

"Certainly. I really appreciate your time. Mr. Whitman said…"

"Okay, Mackenzie. Have a seat right here," Mrs. Smith interrupted. "Now, what is it that you're selling?"

"Well, um, I was hoping to ask you a few questions first," Mackenzie stammered.

"Today I don't have time for questions. Please just get straight to the point," Mrs. Smith directed.

Mackenzie started sweating. "Oh. Okay. Well, um. Let's see here. My company's product is a mobile on-boarding system. Here, let me get you a brochure." Mackenzie opened her portfolio and thought: *This is not going well. How do I turn this around?*

She put OnBoardMobile's brochure on the table and said, "So, Mr. Whitman mentioned that two new hires have recently quit. I know that is not easy on you."

"No, it's not easy. On top of everything else I have to do today, that's the other thing I'll be working on. Reading resumés of young people who have never worked before in their lives." She was looking more disgusted, "Too many parents shelter their kids from the real world. Then the kids get to the real world and can't function. Well, isn't that a surprise."

That did not go the way I wanted it. Strike one. Okay, health, wealth, and relationships. She just mentioned kids, let's go with that. "Do you have children, Mrs. Smith?"

"Me? No. No children."

Strike two, thought Mackenzie. She added, "Oh. So how long have you worked here at Whitman Distributing?"

"Coming up on 15 years," she responded curtly.

"Wow, that's wonderful. Congratulations! Have you always been the HR Director?"

"Mackenzie. I think it's sweet that you're trying to get to know me, but I just don't have time. Can we please cut to the chase, here?"

"Yes, certainly. I apologize. So, as you can see here, this product has proven to save companies money by…" Mackenzie started taking her through the brochure, how Stan had instructed. Three minutes later she ended her quick presentation with, "Now I know that was a lot of information, but if you have any questions, please don't hesitate to contact me. Here's my card."

"Thank you. I don't think we're a good candidate for this technology. I think there would be a steep learning curve and what we have right now is working just fine. I'll walk you out, Mackenzie."

Mackenzie wanted to tell her that the learning curve wasn't steep. With a few staff training sessions, Mackenzie knew she could reduce Karen's paperwork and increase employee productivity. But it felt futile. "Thank you for your time, Mrs. Smith. I really appreciate you meeting with me. If you change your mind, please contact me."

Mackenzie didn't even say goodbye to the receptionist. She didn't think she could get out a word out without her voice cracking from humiliation.

As Mackenzie walked to her car in the Whitman parking lot, she knew that she couldn't go back to the office yet. There was no way she could stand being in a meeting with Stan after that failure. She drove halfway back to the office and then exited the freeway and parked in the nearest empty lot.

That was the worst meeting I have had since starting this job. The worst. This favorable access stuff is a joke. A cruel joke. Mackenzie berated JD's Steps & Rules for the next few minutes. Then she started unloading negative thoughts upon herself, and she began to cry.

That started her on a downward spiral about herself. *Seriously? You're crying? How old are you? Twelve? JD and Bill are wasting their time on you, Mackenzie. You've always prided yourself on your strength, how you can get through anything. And with a simple no, someone shutting the door on you, you can't handle it? You're worthless. You should quit. Go get a job where someone tells you what to do all day. No thinking or risk required.*

She looked at herself in the rearview mirror. Her eyes were red, her face was puffy, her mascara smeared. She grabbed her purse to find a tissue. Next to the tissues was the folded piece of paper that Bill had given her at their last meeting. After she had helped him out of his office chair, they had hobbled over to his file cabinet. Bill grabbed a paper from the file, folded it up, handed it to her and said, "Don't read this today. Take this out and read this when you have a bad moment."

She looked at the folded piece of paper and laughed, "I'd say this qualifies as a bad moment," as she opened up the paper.

The Paradoxical Commandments
Dr. Kent M. Keith

People are illogical, unreasonable, and self-centered.
Love them anyway.

If you do good, people will accuse you of selfish, ulterior motives.
Do good anyway.

If you are successful, you will win false friends and true enemies.
Succeed anyway.

The good you do today will be forgotten tomorrow.
Do good anyway.

Honesty and frankness make you vulnerable.
Be honest and frank anyway.

The biggest men and women with the biggest ideas can be shot down by the smallest men and women with the smallest minds.
Think big anyway.

People favor underdogs but follow only top dogs.
Fight for a few underdogs anyway.

What you spend years building may be destroyed overnight.
Build anyway.

People really need help but may attack you if you do help them.
Help people anyway.

Give the world the best you have and you'll get kicked in the teeth.
Give the world the best you have anyway.

Mackenzie finally breathed a deep breath as she read the last two lines. *Well, I feel like I got kicked in the teeth today, Bill. But I'm not the only one who has had her teeth kicked in.* She thought about

Bill's stories. He had lost more than his entire financial worth and then in an effort to earn his way out, he literally got kicked in the teeth and destroyed on the football field before he could collect a paycheck. Mackenzie took another deep breath and thought, *I think I can take a little kick to the teeth. After all, now I know a good dentist.*

Mackenzie smiled at the thought and took a look at her teeth in the rearview mirror. Out loud she said, "Yep, I still have my teeth." She grinned. Then she remembered something Bill had also said, "When you get knocked down it's okay to stay down for a moment and catch your breath. But, you don't do yourself or anyone else any good if you stay down. You gotta look up and get up."

She shook her head and continued, "You thought that was going to be an easy win, Mackenzie. You hadn't committed to excellent practice before that meeting. You weren't prepared for anything but an easy yes. Sure, that meeting sucked. But it's not the worst one you'll have. You've had much worse things happen in your life. So look up and get up."

She turned on the music in the car and drove back to the office. Mackenzie was relieved that Stan was on the phone when she returned. She logged her sales call and then looked through her notes from JD. She decided she would join the group cycling ride on Saturday, the next morning. She wasn't sure if JD rode on Saturday mornings, but if he did, she wanted to ask him a few questions.

LOGIC AND INTUITION
Chapter 24

Mackenzie arrived early and sat down in the coffee shop at a table near the window. She watched outside eagerly, her eyes scanning the pavement for JD. Finally, she spotted him. He was still unloading his bike from his car, so she ran out to meet him.

"JD. Can I please tell you about a scenario and ask you what I did wrong?" Mackenzie pleaded.

"Well, good morning to you. Can I pump up my tires first?" he joked. "Go ahead."

Mackenzie launched in, "So I gained favorable access with the CEO of a company...I did my research and decided that the HR Director was my best prospect...then, as you suggested, I sent a concise email to the CEO, then he forwarded my email to the HR Director, so I wrote her an email...then the HR Director emailed me late on Thursday night for a ten minute meeting on Friday morning...I made it to her office on time...but she didn't give me the time of day...I tried asking her questions, and she kept cutting me off then told me she wasn't interested and walked me to the door." Mackenzie took an audible breath, "So, where did I go wrong?"

"What happened to 'go slow to go fast'?" JD asked incredulously.

"I didn't have time for that," Mackenzie blurted.

JD raised his eyebrows, "Tell me. How strong was your favorable access to the CEO?"

"Am I supposed to answer this?" Mackenzie asked as she recalled Rule 2.

"No, you don't have to. I'll tell you. You only had general access. You thought you knew the CEO and he barely remembered you. Strong favorable access compels the CEO to talk to the HR Director about you, but general access has very limited pull. He probably didn't even write anything on the forwarded email."

Mackenzie nodded sadly.

JD reiterated, "Strong favorable access can grant the power of referrals. Your first mis-step. And how many deposits did you make into the HR Director's account before meeting with her?"

Mackenzie was silent and inwardly cringed.

"Your second mis-step. Remember that slow-fast thing. Everyone is on a tight time schedule, which makes it even more important for you to bring value to the other person. Make it worth her time. You can't skip the Steps & Rules because of your own time constraint. It's not about you. It's about your prospect.

"You don't automatically get favorable access because you know someone she knows, even if it is her boss. You have to earn the opportunity for favorable access. Before you walk into her office, she has to know who you are in a favorable way. She has to know that you appreciate her time and her position. You have to bring her something of value. You can't just tell her that without showing her that through your actions and sincerity. Did you at least leave the meeting by making her day better?"

Mackenzie remained silent. Although she was getting put in

her place, JD's gentle tone let her know that these were mistakes many people made.

"And what was your expectation of what would happen at this meeting?" JD asked.

Mackenzie laid it out honestly, "I thought she would express interest in my product. I thought I had followed the Steps."

"Your third mis-step. You think that just by checking off certain steps…POOF! Magic sale. That doesn't happen. If that were the case, everyone would follow these steps and call it a sales formula. This isn't a formula where steps $1 + 2 + 3 = 6$. The sales process is both logic and intuition."

JD held his hands, palms facing up in front of him, raising one hand with logic and the other hand with intuition. "The logical, factual side is knowing your product inside and out and knowing the probable outcomes of using your product and how it applies to your customer's business."

JD continued, "The intuitive side of sales is figuring out what they are saying when their answers are often hidden in the middle of their sentences. You ask questions to reveal your customers' needs and apply their answers to where you can add value to your customer and their business. Intuition doesn't follow a formula, but there is a general process. You push to get yourself into position, pull with the right questions to find out what they really want or need, push with your knowledge about their business, and pull with intense listening. With favorable access you are allowed to connect their thoughts with their possibilities."

Mackenzie recognized the rhythm. Push, pull, push, pull. She kept pushing and forgetting to pull, just like her first group rides. *It's hard to remember to pull when I'm so used to pushing. I have to practice the full circle.*

JD put his hands down and spoke again, "In the early situations where I hadn't taken the time to make deposits and achieve the strongest favorable access, I learned to let go of my expectations and focus solely on the person across the table.

"I'll give you one early career example. I was in a lawyer's office, and the lawyer became calmly detached, clearly not hearing a word I was saying. So I said, 'Ya know, let me throw this brochure in the trash. I respect your time too much to show you things you may already know. I promised to be out of here in fifteen minutes. I saw a specialty coffeehouse on my way in here. If I leave right now, I can bring you your favorite cup of coffee and be right back so you can get ready for your next client meeting.'" JD gave Mackenzie a half-smile, "When I returned with four cups of coffee, one for each of his staff, I thanked him for teaching me that I had a lot to learn. He thanked me. And I noticed he had pulled my brochure out of the trash."

JD continued, "I did not make a sale that day, but I made an impression with the deposit. You have to take the time to make the deposits."

"I can see that now." Mackenzie nodded, then added, "But, besides me running to get coffee for everyone, what other kind of deposits can I make?"

"Mackenzie, it wasn't about the coffee. It was about the respect for his time at that moment. I wasn't following the Steps at that point. I was following my intuition."

Mackenzie paused. She realized that she was only thinking of herself and her outcome at the meeting with Karen Smith. It was doomed from the start. "So, did I totally mess up that relationship? Or do you think I could get a second chance?"

"Although you aren't quite ready for it, I'll share Rule 1 with you. This will help you figure out how to re-start that relationship." JD paused as Mackenzie got ready to take notes.

"I'm putting a lot of trust in you by telling you this. This is not to be manipulated. If you manipulate this, you will burn your relationships and reputation to the ground." JD looked intently at Mackenzie, making sure she understood the importance of what he just said.

Mackenzie nodded solemnly.

JD's tone was serious, "Rule 1 is: You can't get what you want until they get what they want."

RULE 1: *You can't get what you want until they get what they want.*

Mackenzie wrote down his words and thought, *That seems obvious. Why is that such a big deal?*

JD answered her unspoken question, "At first, this seems simple. But in order to do this well, it takes a great amount of humility. This is much harder than it sounds. To follow Rule 1 well, you have to put aside your own desire to appear smart, to take credit, and to feel in control. This brings us back to the Steps."

"STEPS" OF THE SALES PROCESS

Step 1: Understand your general access.
Step 2: Develop a plan to gain favorable access.
Step 3: Leverage favorable access to get a meeting.

"RULES" OF THE PACELINE

Rule 1: <u>You can't get what you want until they get what they want.</u>
Rule 2: Go slow to go fast.
Rule 3: Questions are rarely questions. Understand the why.
Rule 4: Make significant deposits before withdrawing or asking for a loan.
Rule 5: Practice until the process becomes instinctive.

CUSTOMER CENTERED
Chapter 25

JD summarized, "Step 1: General access to Step 2: Favorable access. Step 3: Favorable access to get a meeting. You know these. Before we add the next two, let me ask you a question, and I do want to know your answer." JD asked, "Mackenzie, with the ten minutes you had, tell me, what did you ask the HR Director?"

"Well, first I tried to ask her a few questions about her, to find out how I could add value to her wealth, her health, and her relationships, but she cut me off and said she didn't have time for questions."

"Hold up. When did I suggest that you utilize small talk and personal questions?" JD asked sternly.

Mackenzie then realized her mistake, "Oh. Right. This was a business meeting. This was where I needed to focus on asking questions about work, not personal small talk questions."

"Exactly. Big mis-step there. Timing of these conversations is important and how you approach a business conversation is important. Did you set any expectations before walking into that meeting?"

"No. I thought I needed to develop trust first," Mackenzie sighed.

"One of the strongest ways to develop trust in a business meeting is to design and send an agenda before the meeting. Then at the meeting, you walk through the agenda, and you ask, 'Is there any particular place you would like to start or anything you would like to add to this agenda?'

"This is Step 4: Set the agenda and then put the customer in control."

STEP 4: *Set the agenda and then put the customer in control.*

JD waited for her to finish her notes, and then continued, "If you set an agenda and keep the control of the meeting, your prospect starts to feel out of control. When people feel out of control, they feel fear. When they feel fear, they will respond negatively towards you so that they can retain some form of control. Give your prospect the control so that she can relax and enter into dialogue with you."

Mackenzie shook her head, "Put the customer in control. That is the opposite of what I've been trained to do."

JD laughed and replied, "Yep. You've been trained to steer the conversation towards how your product will solve all of her problems. She doesn't care about your product. She cares about what she has to do that day. Your agenda has to address her needs then you give your prospect the ability to control the next steps. People are told what to do and when to do it. All. Day. Long. It feels good to be in control! Give your customer the confidence that you are thinking about her needs, not yours."

Mackenzie nodded, "Okay, that makes sense. But agendas seem so formal. Do I really need an agenda for a first meeting?"

"Yes, absolutely you need an agenda at your first meeting. Most people, because of limited time, want to know what to expect from a meeting. Before any activity, we have to prepare mentally and physically.

"Whether we are going to spend our morning with others on a cycling ride or in a business meeting, we prepare with the right clothing, equipment, and mindset; otherwise we'll be at a disadvantage from the start. You know where you want to go and have a process for how to get there. If you ride solo, you do this mentally. If you need someone to come along for the ride, you explain the direction of where you are going. For both of you to get something out of the ride, you need to set the expectations and understand how dialogue and group dynamics work. You have this basic process in a cycling ride and a business meeting. Before every business meeting, you design and send an agenda to set the expectations."

Mackenzie pulled up her notes on her phone and began typing.

"Let's start with the agenda. The format of your agenda should have the format of any good story: History, Dark Side, Discovery, and Simple Solution." JD emphasized the key words as he spoke, "*History*. Highlight your prospect's business and ask your questions for how they've succeeded thus far. *Dark Side*. Using your knowledge of their company, bullet point your assumptions about their industry and general trends you've noticed. *Discovery*. Ask your prospect to challenge your assumptions, get them to talk further about key areas that may lead to more questions. *Simple Solution*. Remind them of their answers and guide them to come up with a solution which clearly defines their problem.

"Your goal with any meeting, but the first meeting, in particular, is to build trust. When you give the control of the conversation over to your prospect, then you are the initiator of building the trust. When you ask your prospect where she would like to start, most often, prospects will start at the top of the agenda. If you've done your homework on your prospect's company history, you can open the conversation focused on the company's history and ask her what other important points she would add to the history of her company. You do not need to go in knowing everything about her company, just enough to let her know that you are interested in her company's needs. Beginning this way allows you to enter into Step 5: Build trust through dialogue.

STEP 5: *Build trust through dialogue.*

JD paused and then continued, "It's hard to do any business without trust. The most basic way to develop trust is through dialogue with Rules 1, 2, 3, and 4 in mind."

Mackenzie rehearsed the first four rules in her mind:

Rule 1: You can't get what you want until they get what they want.
Rule 2: Go slow to go fast.
Rule 3: Questions are rarely questions. Find the why.
Rule 4: Make deposits before withdrawing or asking for a loan.

JD let his words sink in before starting again, "So, you've done the legwork, and you've set the agenda with her in mind. Now, you let her steer the next steps, and you listen carefully, asking questions to better understand her perspective, her job tools, and her professional headaches so that you can see where you might bring value. Does that make sense?"

"Yes, it does make sense." Mackenzie couldn't help but add, "But it's a lot of work. Does all of this really make a difference?"

JD raised his eyebrows again, saying without words, *you know the answer to that.*

Mackenzie quickly replied, "Don't answer that. I know it does. I just have a lot of work to do. Thank you, JD. And it's time to ride now, huh?"

"Yep. Sure is. Make the ride count, Mackenzie."

Mackenzie nodded and replied, "Will do."

"STEPS" OF THE SALES PROCESS

Step 1: Understand your general access.
Step 2: Develop a plan to gain favorable access.
Step 3: Leverage favorable access to get a meeting.
Step 4: Set the agenda and then put the customer in control.
Step 5: Build trust through dialogue.

"RULES" OF THE PACELINE

Rule 1: You can't get what you want until they get what they want.
Rule 2: Go slow to go fast.
Rule 3: Questions are rarely questions. Understand the why.
Rule 4: Make significant deposits before withdrawing or asking for a loan.
Rule 5: Practice until the process becomes instinctive.

GAME PLAN PREPARATION
Chapter 26

Mackenzie thought about JD's Steps throughout the bike ride and felt overwhelmed by how much prework she needed to do before her next meeting. She decided to ride directly to work after the ride, thinking, *it'll be quiet on a Saturday morning and I can take my time researching my general access. Then I can figure out my game plan for how to make the right deposits in order to build trust.*

She swiped her security card once she arrived at the office and took her bike with her up the elevator. She spent the next few hours making her lists of potential contacts and creating a web of connections using her social media tools. She was thankful that she had invested time making connections on social media and was pleasantly surprised that her network was larger than she realized, even if the social media contacts were only in her general access. Her contacts held mostly low-level positions in the various companies, but she reminded herself to go slow now in order to go fast later.

In her research, she found that a number of her potential suspects from the cold call lists, given to her by management, had links with Stan, her sales manager. She double-backed on

Stan's pipeline and was confused as to why he hadn't pursued certain leads. The contacts weren't even entered in his Sales Excellence System. She wrote down a few of his key contacts, researched their interests and resolved to ask Stan about them. *But what was the best way to ask?*

She looked at her notes from JD, particularly the first four Steps & Rules. She thought about what Stan might want at work and in life. She had heard through the grapevine that the only reason Stan took the Sales Manager job was that he was promised the promotion and title of VP when the sales crew reached their first year sales goals. Titles were important to Stan and feeling respected was even more important to him.

How can I help him to feel respected? And have I made enough deposits in order to ask for a withdrawal? The short answer to that one was definitely a No. *So, how can I make deposits without looking completely inauthentic?*

It was getting close to noon, and she was hungry. The extra energy bar in her desk drawer did not look appetizing to her. She closed down her computer and carried her bike back to the elevator.

As the elevator doors opened for her, she and her bike stepped forward and slammed into a man walking out of the elevator. She and Stan exchanged surprised expressions. Stan, wiping off his jeans from the tire dirt, talked first, "Mackenzie. I'm shocked to see you here since I never see you during the week." His sarcastic smirk spread from his mouth to his eyes, daring her to respond.

Mackenzie's mind had been running through ways to show respect for Stan and knew this was her first chance. "Stan! I owe you an explanation for my absence from the office and my lack of Sales Excellence input. Is now a good time for you?"

"I only have a few minutes. If you would have been at the last sales meeting, you'd know that I'm preparing for our CEO meeting on Monday," he jabbed.

"Yes, of course. Again, I apologize for missing the sales meeting. Would it be helpful if I made a reservation for you and the CEO to have lunch on Monday?"

"That's been taken care of already. What I really need you to do is to log in your sales calls so that I can pull a final report and make sure everything's in order before our CEO starts firing people."

"Absolutely, I did that this morning. I'm trying to use my work days for making calls and after hours for doing paperwork. I am trying to follow your advice with networking. I already see your wisdom in making that recommendation. Clearly, I have a lot to learn from you, and I really appreciate your knowledge and experience with sales." She knew she was stretching the truth, but he had harped on the crew to network, so it wasn't an outright lie.

Stan straightened up, ever so slightly. His expression softened from pure disdain and tiptoed towards approval. "Thanks. Yes, you do have a lot to learn, Mackenzie. I'm pleasantly surprised that you are finally doing what I've been asking you to do for months."

Mackenzie let the slight again roll by and continued, "Stan, you've told us that you are still responsible for your own sales goals as well as managing the sales crew, which I'm sure is a heavy burden. This morning, I researched a number of leads generated from the cold call lists you gave us. Would it be helpful to your own sales network if I sent you the information of the contacts with whom you are connected?"

Stan looked puzzled. "That's an interesting thought. You're right; it is a large burden to manage you and the crew. No offense, but I often feel like I'm babysitting a bunch of preschoolers."

"Well, thanks for attaching our training wheels, Stan," Mackenzie joked.

Stan laughed, and a slight smile showed up on his face, "Good one. So, tell me quickly. What did you find?"

Mackenzie walked him through her research.

Stan perked up with one particular contact, but downplayed it, "Mackenzie, a few of these contacts might be interesting to follow-up, but most of these accounts are way too small for me. They aren't worth my time."

"Oh. Hmmm. Well, like you've told us, no matter what the size, we need to stay top of mind to our prospects. Is there a chance you could lead me with an introduction and I could follow-up for you?"

"Mackenzie. I'm not going to open the door for you on my own contacts. My job is to teach you my methods, not to do the work for you."

Mackenzie regretted how she asked her question. This was supposed to be a time for her to help him. With one question, she had messed it all up. She tried to back-pedal.

"Stan, I didn't mean it like that. I've just been learning that business relationships take time to build, and if I can make deposits into relationships on your behalf or on behalf of the company, you could benefit in the long run."

"Mackenzie, no offense, but I don't need your help. My sales numbers are fine. I need you to work on yours."

"Understood. Will do. See you tomorrow." And with that, she pushed the button to the elevator and was thankful it arrived immediately.

LIVING WITH HUMILITY
Chapter 27

Mackenzie pushed her pedals hard to relieve the stress after her failed conversation with Stan. She had lost her appetite for lunch and instead took a different route home to pass by Reichardt's Clothing Store.

She wondered how Bill would respond to the situation with her manager. She decided she'd see if Bill had time to talk and was grateful that he did.

After a few minutes of pleasantries, she asked, "Bill, when people told you they wouldn't help you, what did you do?"

"Mackenzie, first off, you have to understand that no one owes you anything. No one owes you their help.

"Some people go through life thinking that all of the people around them owe them something. They walk around taking what they can, holding on tightly to what they have, and end up carrying a pile of stuff around wherever they go: titles, money, ego. I call that 'being full of it.' At first, that pile you're carrying makes you look bigger and stronger. But then all that pile of pride does is start to get rather heavy and weigh you down.

"There are others who understand they don't deserve any of it. They are grateful for what they do have and recognize how others helped them along the way. That's called living with humility. They recognize the value of others, no matter how big or how small.

"Now, I started off out of college as a puffed up pile of pride. I walked around in my own strength and didn't need anyone's help...until the line quit blocking for me and life starting hitting me in the face. 'Pride goes before destruction and an arrogant spirit before a fall.'

"I sit here today knowing that the only way I got to where I wanted to go was by the help of other people. This is why I help as many people as I can. What goes around comes around. I owe a lot of people for my success."

"If you don't mind, Bill, can you give me a few examples of people who helped you?" Mackenzie asked.

Bill replied, "I'd love to. Let's see, there are so many. My mom, Ethel. She was a tough ol' bird, never quit working and never let me quit. She lit a fire under me in athletics and business. But I think you're asking me about help from people other than my family."

Mackenzie nodded and Bill responded, "The General Manager of Firestone Tires. The GM saw potential in me and placed me in a position to coach the first Iowa Little All-American Football League. That move re-started my sports shop. Then there were the kids that I coached in the football league, from both sides of the track. They taught me the most about life. The parents of some of those kids; they introduced me to my next set of customers and influencers. Then, there was Bob Dillon, who gave me a sentence that stuck with people. He taught me about the power of advertising. And many more. But I think I'll start with those. That sound good?"

Mackenzie nodded her approval and Bill continued, "Let's see. The GM of Firestone Tires. I met the GM when I was peddling I-caps. He knew I used to be a football star; he had followed my college football career in the papers. On one occasion, he asked me about what my plans were after the Hawks' winning 1956 season ended and if I was going to continue with the Sports Shop. He told me, without mincing words, 'Bill, people forget that you were a football star almost as soon as you leave the field. Have you ever thought of getting back on the field as a football coach?'

"'Coaching who?' I asked him. At the time, I thought he was referring to college football, which I had no interest in doing.

"He answered, 'Kids. Middle school kids.'

"Now, I wasn't what you'd call a nurturing type, and I was better at making kids cry, especially my own. The GM had a son in middle school, and I had no interest in babysitting his kid or any other rich kids. 'Nah, I don't think that's for me.' I told him.

"But he had planted a seed. Pop Warner football was up and coming in the late 50s. With the University of Iowa winning the Rose Bowl, the local kids were getting more interested in the game. I didn't know it then, but it's clear to me now, that the GM had something specific in mind. He took about a year of watering that idea-seed and helped me to see myself as a coach.

"You see, the GM had a problem and an idea of how to solve that problem. But just like anything that takes money or time, you have to sell the idea to others in order to make it happen. I ran into him a few times in the next few months, and he invited me out to the Firestone Tires manufacturing plant. He said I'd be doing him a big favor if I came out to the plant to meet a few Iowa football fans.

"I really thought I was doing him a favor. Ha! It was his way of getting me out there to see his vision. After he had me shake hands with a few workers and sign a few footballs, he took me to the empty field behind the property. It was one o'clock in the afternoon, and there was a handful of rough looking pre-teenage boys smoking cigarettes. He told me that these kids were skipping school, didn't have anywhere else to go, and were probably the kids who were vandalizing his building. He said, 'Ya know what I think Bill? I think that what these kids need is a sport with a coach they respect.' And I walked right into that because that's what I needed when I was ten and my parents were working non-stop at the Café.

"I responded, 'Yeah, and two of those kids look like linebackers. I bet ya they'd hit like a truck. And that one there in the red shirt looks like an athlete.' So I asked the GM, 'Hey, what are you doing with that last football you've got?' as I pointed to the football he had in his hands. The GM handed the ball to me and nodded.

"I took that football, walked close to those kids, raised the football in the air and said, 'Whoever catches this ball can keep it. Who's in?' They elbowed each other and looked me up and down. They tossed their cigarettes, and all five of them lifted their chins signaling to me that they were taking up the challenge. I told them to run back for 15 yards. I spiraled the ball, and they all scrambled for it. The kid in the red shirt dove and made a killer catch. Seeing him throw his body like that made me think back to my first catch as a kid trying to impress the older kids playing ball outside the gates of the University of Iowa. I just wanted a chance to prove I was worth something.

"I yelled to the red shirt, 'Nice catch.' Red shirt was beaming. So I asked them, 'You guys wanna run a few plays?'

"Red jogged over to me, and the other guys followed. I took a knee, gave them positions, and showed them my favorite play from the Packers. We ran that play three times and said, 'Now, I want to see you run it, Red.' After that, I took a stick and drew two more plays in the dirt. Then I asked the two who looked like linebackers, 'Who wants to try to tackle me?' One took a run at me, I dropped my shoulder and knocked him to the ground. The second charged, and I knocked him on top of the other one. 'You wanna learn how to run like the pros?' I asked them.

"'Yeah!' they replied as they dusted themselves off.

"'Alright. Meet me here next Wednesday, same time. I'll

teach you how to tackle like it matters. And Red,' I said as I tossed the ball to the kid in the red shirt, 'Learn those next two plays I scratched in the dirt. See you next Wednesday.' Red caught the ball, and his eyes lit up.

"I started back to the GM and told him, 'That was the most fun I've had since I quit playing.'

"The GM said, 'Bill, I'm guessing you're the first man who has taken time out of his day to give those kids something to look forward to. You've got a real gift with tough kids.'

"Huh. I had never thought about that. 'Well,' I said to the GM, 'I'm meeting them here next Wednesday. You okay with me using your field?'

"'It's yours,' he said and added, 'Bill, I brought you out here for a reason. I'd like you to start up a Little All-American Football League and here's why and what you need to consider…'

"The GM got me thinking bigger than one more practice with a handful of street kids. He tied coaching football to being a sports influence in Des Moines. He told me how to mix the haves with the have-nots by giving them a level playing field and a common goal. He told me about how his wealthy and influential friends wanted their kids in a football league. And he told me that those wealthy parents would need a sports shop to buy football gear and had the ability to subsidize gear for the kids who couldn't afford it."

COMMUNICATE EFFECTIVELY
Chapter 28

Bill leaned forward, "You see, he used JD's Rule 1: 'You can't get what you want until they get what they want.' The GM wanted the street kids off of the empty lot behind his plant. He wanted to stop the vandalism. And he wanted his own son to play football with me as his coach. But he couldn't get what he wanted by demanding that I do it. He used a technique that JD spells out in his rules. Rule 6 is: Communicate the value of your vision in their terms.

RULE 6: *Communicate the value of your vision in their terms.*

"The GM tied my story to the stories of the street kids. He knew it would take a lot of my time, so he made sure to communicate how the value of this time investment would benefit me and my business in the long run.

"He brought me to the field with a football and an opportunity to interact. He observed how I interacted with those kids and communicated the value that I brought to those kids in a way I couldn't see from my perspective.

"Rule 6 is tied closely with Rule 7: Provide perspective, not just content.

RULE 7: *Provide perspective not just content.*

The GM saw something in me that I didn't see in myself. I was just trying to keep my head above water with selling those I-caps. I had been rubbing elbows with the social elites, but I didn't know how to translate an I-cap sale to a sports shop customer. I knew I didn't want to keep peddling those caps. Instead, I wanted to have a successful sports shop.

"We all have blind spots in our own lives because we're too close to our own problems. That GM saw my life from a different perspective. He saw a need and how I could fill the need and simultaneously be fulfilled by it because he had taken the time to get to know me. That afternoon, he taught me the importance of providing perspective, not just content.

"The GM told me his thoughts, asked me some questions, and then said, 'Think about it, Bill. Let me know your answer by next Wednesday.'

"The GM knew that I brought the football cred, and I was tough enough not to be intimidated by street kids or the demanding parents of the rich kids. He knew that by giving my time, I could increase my influence, impact, and demand-pull. As JD would say, I could develop favorable access with the people I wanted as customers. But the GM also knew that I'd ultimately fail if I was only coaching because of what I'd get from it. I had to have a passion to help both those who couldn't afford the gear and those who could. I had to have the passion for coaching in order to devote the time required to teach a bunch of unruly boys.

"You always have to check your motives. When you find yourself prioritizing money and influence over valuing people, you will fail at whatever you're trying to achieve.

"I gave that ball to Red as my first promise that I'd do what I said I'd do. That next Wednesday I didn't let anything stop me from being at that field on time. Teddy Roosevelt said it best, and JD made it into Rule 8: People don't care how much you know until they know how much you care."

RULE 8: "People don't care how much you know until they know how much you care." - Theodore Roosevelt

---

Bill continued, "Those were some great kids, and they taught me more about life than I ever taught them on the field."

Mackenzie felt drawn to find out more about the kids and wondered if their lives changed because of Bill's influence. "Wow, Bill. It sounds like you really poured yourself into those kids. So, did a lot of them end up playing football in high school or even college?"

"STEPS" OF THE SALES PROCESS

Step 1: Understand your general access.
Step 2: Develop a plan to gain favorable access.
Step 3: Leverage favorable access to get a meeting.
Step 4: Set the agenda and then put the customer in control.
Step 5: Build trust through dialogue.

"RULES" OF THE PACELINE

Rule 1: You can't get what you want until they get what they want.
Rule 2: Go slow to go fast.
Rule 3: Questions are rarely questions. Understand the why.
Rule 4: Make significant deposits before withdrawing or asking for a loan.
Rule 5: Practice until the process becomes instinctive.
Rule 6: <u>Communicate the value of your vision in their terms.</u>
Rule 7: <u>Provide perspective not just content.</u>
Rule 8: <u>People don't care how much you know until they know how much you care.</u>

PART THREE

Discovery

BEHIND THE SCENES
Chapter 29

Bill considered her question and answered, "Well, some kids did go on to play in high school and college. Some became great successes in life. But street life and street influence have their own strong pull. We all want each hard-knock story to end with the Rose Bowl. In different seasons of life, new problems spring up and get in the way of your vision and priorities. A few years into coaching, I asked one of my squads, 'Who's the toughest kid in school?' They answered, 'Lloyd! Lloyd's the toughest kid.' I asked, 'Why isn't he out here playing football with us?' They told me, 'Lloyd said he ain't playing.' So I asked, 'Where is Lloyd?' They told me that he was at the Willkie House, which was a space dedicated to social services in the inner city.

"I went to the Willkie House after practice, and Lloyd was sitting there at the end of a cement slab with a half-inflated basketball tucked under his chin. I said, 'Come on Lloyd, come on out and play football with us.'

"He barely raised his eyes and mumbled, 'Mister, I ain't playin' football.'

"I said, 'Here's your helmet, here's your jersey, here are

some shoes. Take 'em. If you want to play, then come out and join us.' This was on a Wednesday. On a Saturday morning at 9 o'clock, down this little dirt lane behind Firestone Tire, this Lloyd comes walking down the path.

"'Here comes Lloyd! Here comes Lloyd!' the team shouted.

"Lloyd had walked from south of the freeway clear out behind the Firestone Tire plant to play, which was over three miles. To make a long story short, he became a leader of the team on offense and defense. He was voted as captain. And when the season was over, I called his middle school, and I asked how the kid was doing, thinking that he would have improved in school after seeing his leadership on the field. She said, 'He's failing. He won't even be able to go on to high school.'

"Well, I was disappointed, but I was too busy to worry about Lloyd in those days. A couple of years later I saw that he was picked up for stealing a car. And a couple of years after that, I saw where he was involved in a burglary where a policeman was shot and killed. And Lloyd went to prison for life."

Bill shook his head slowly. Mackenzie's mouth dropped unexpectedly. She didn't know how to respond.

Bill finally continued, "About six years later, there was another kid that was almost identical to Lloyd. Captain and leader of the team, lived in the same area, went to the same middle school. And at the end of the season, I called the school and asked, 'How's Frank getting along?'

"'Franklin is doing so poorly that we classify him as educationally retarded.' And I said, 'Wait a minute. Wait a minute! I was too busy six years ago. I'm not too busy now.'

"I called a woman I knew on the school board; she got ahold of the superintendent of the school. They took the kid out of the classroom and gave him remedial reading skills for four months, and they brought his reading level from second grade to eighth grade. He went on to the Technical High School in Des Moines and got a scholarship to play basketball at a small college. He graduated from college, got married, got a nice job, had a few kids, and lives in a wonderful neighborhood.

"And the difference between those two lives…" Bill's voice cracked with emotion. "Mackenzie, the difference between those two lives is one phone call from somebody who cared."

The last four words echoed in Mackenzie's mind, *from somebody who cared.*

The words pierced her heart, and she felt a little sick. Here she was, feeling sorry for herself that her manager wouldn't open a few doors for her like she thought he should. *What am I doing for someone else and not worrying about the return? How am I helping anyone other than myself?*

She hadn't re-engaged with the Big Brother Big Sister program since she graduated. She didn't have time. No, she hadn't made the time. She focused back on Bill and said, "Bill, you have a big heart. But how did you make time for so many other people?"

"When we step out and help someone else, we gain perspective. We learn more by helping others than we do by helping ourselves. I think life is about learning and growing, and if by helping others I learn more and grow faster, then essentially, helping others is multiplying my time."

Mackenzie had never thought of helping others in the way that Bill stated it. *Helping others multiplied his time. That is an interesting way to look at something that I thought was taking my time,* she thought.

Bill continued, "You'll also notice that I didn't just go to anyone to help Frank. Had I made that first call to someone I didn't know then there likely wouldn't be enough momentum to get anywhere. I went to someone within my favorable access, a trusted friend. I told her Lloyd's story. Then, I told her Frank's back-story. I told her about the immense progress Frank had made that year. She knew I was pulling for Frank, and I made it easy for her to want to pull for him too.

"She then took those stories to someone within her sphere of influence, someone in her favorable access. Together, we created a paceline draft for Frank. Frank still had to do the work. No one was going to learn to read for him. He had to put in the effort and trust it was worth it."

Mackenzie nodded. She started to see the process. It wasn't just a phone call from someone who cared. The work behind the scenes allowed that phone call to form a paceline for Frank. Bill had made tremendous deposits into Frank as his coach. Frank learned to trust Bill. Bill created favorable access with Frank. Bill used his favorable access with a friend on the school board to create a demand-pull for Frank. The friend used her favorable access with the superintendent to get Frank set up for tutoring. But Frank still had to do the work. Even in the draft, he had to push and pull hard to keep up.

Bill could see that Mackenzie was starting to connect the Steps & Rules.

CRAFT YOUR MESSAGE
Chapter 30

Bill echoed Mackenzie's thoughts, "Pulling one kid towards a different future took a whole paceline of people getting aligned. It's always a lot more involved than it looks on the surface. And most attempts don't succeed the way we want them to. Frank wasn't the only kid we gathered a paceline team around, but he was one kid who did succeed; his success helped us to know that all the effort could be worth it. It's the same story in business.

"My friend, Bob Dillon, had worked on thousands of radio advertisements over the decades in his career. Hundreds of those ads failed miserably. But each time they failed, he learned what he needed to change, and he practiced until the process became instinctive. After each failure, he honed his customers' message better the next time. By the time I met him, Bob Dillon could craft a message that stuck in people's heads like a Bob Dylan song.

"Bob had watched my inventory transition slowly over the decades from sports gear to men's quality clothing. Just because you think you've made wise business decisions doesn't mean that your customers will agree with you. Reichardt's Quality

Clothing Store was struggling when Bob walked in one day and said to me, 'You know, Bill, most store owners are absent from the sales floor, but there *is* a Mr. Reichardt, and he *is* in the store.'

"Bob Dillon sat me down and questioned me about what made Reichardt's store different. Why would someone buy a $500 Southwick suit from Reichardt's instead of going down the street to buy a generic suit for $100 that looked similar on the hanger? Bob Dillon helped me craft my message to tell prospects what made us different and why. Our first TV commercial and nearly every advertisement since then has had me saying the same message."

Bill straightened his back and turned to the side slightly as if he were being filmed:

"Today at Reichardt's we hold to the same fundamental belief we had when we opened for business: Only satisfied customers become permanent customers. Nearly 80% of our business is repeat business. We keep our trade...

"No sale is ever final here. We have courteous and competent personnel here. We guarantee your complete satisfaction when you shop here. And I'll see to it. Because I'm here. I'm Bill Reichardt, and I own the store."

Mackenzie recited his tagline silently in her head along with Bill. *Because I'm here. I'm Bill Reichardt, and I own the store.* Even though she had never shopped there, that commercial made her think she could trust the old man who said he owned the store. Mackenzie recalled JD saying, 'It's hard to do any business without trust.'"

Bill continued, "People love to buy, but hate to be forced into it. When someone has enough trust to buy, they feel good about their purchase. It was essential for us that our customers felt good about their purchase because I said 'No sale is ever final.' And I meant it. I had to have my customers fully satisfied; otherwise, I'd have a return rack of custom-tailored suits that I wouldn't ever be able to re-sell. It was a risk to make a statement like that. But it paid dividends because our repeat customers developed deep loyalty; they knew that we would always take care of them. We learned their names. We knew their stories. We made them feel known.

"And my message was known after a few years of that TV ad. I lived, breathed, and stood by that message for over 40 years. After that first commercial where Bob Dillon helped me to own my message and enlightened me on the virtues of advertising, my business increased six-fold. I was finally able to make good on that comment that I actually owned the store."

"Just like that?" Mackenzie asked, incredulous. "You started advertising, and you increased your business six-fold?"

Bill smiled. "Nope. Advertising is just a method. Advertising, marketing, branding, public relations, testimonials, referrals...they are all just methods...to gain better favorable access and create demand-pull."

Mackenzie felt her mind suddenly open with ideas. "This is really starting to make sense, Bill! I've always thought that those methods were just to get brand recognition. But you're right; it's to get a more personal connection. People love to buy so you create demand-pull to buy. Favorable access opens the door, and creating demand-pull encourages them to buy! Bill, as I'm listening to you, I can't help but think that more people need to hear what you are saying and hear it directly from you and JD. I feel like I'm getting a college degree in sales just by listening to you two. I heard that you are about to sell the store. Is that correct?"

Bill nodded.

"Have you ever considered packaging your store sale with training for employees through your stories and lessons?" Mackenzie asked.

"Wayne, my friend buying the store, put a few of my talks, speeches, and commercials onto the World Wide Web somewhere. I've told the other stories so often to Wayne that I'm sure he could tell them verbatim if he wanted to."

Mackenzie disagreed, "Bill, you have a unique way of communicating through your stories that would benefit all sales employees. Because most of the new store's employees know of you and your ties with this chain of clothing stores, the employees will be that much more engaged with your message. You've walked in their shoes. Do you and Wayne have a similar perspective on sales?"

"Yes and no," Bill answered. "Wayne operates a chain of stores; I only operated one store for over 40 years. Wayne is nicer to his employees and has a calmer demeanor. But as far as sales, I think most business owners' have some natural sales skills and don't necessarily think that others need training. Tell me what you are thinking."

Mackenzie felt like she was on a roll and ventured, "Let me ask you one more question. Has it been easy or hard to attract and retain quality employees?"

Bill replied, "My employees have been long-term. For the most part, I haven't had a problem retaining my long-term employees, but I've seen it become more difficult to bring on new people. They just don't have the longstanding loyalty like other generations."

"That's not surprising to hear," Mackenzie affirmed. "My company has tracked a number of trends with various industries, and the results are similar across the board. Bill, I haven't told you what I sell, but basically, it's a way for employers to engage their employees through training videos on their mobile devices. It's like having human resources and training in the palm of your hand, teaching individual employees what they need to know, with the ability to view the video as many times as they want or need so that they can learn at their own speed. Then, they are held accountable for learning and incorporating the material into their sales process efforts. We've also found that employees become more engaged when top management shares a snippet of their personal story and a lesson they have learned with their employee base. I'm thinking that Wayne's stores and employees could really benefit from hearing your stories on a mobile learning platform. What do you think?"

"Mackenzie, you're asking good questions as you're looking to add value and to get my buy-in. As you know, I sold clothing. When someone walked through that door, there was a high probability that the person wanted to buy something because he was already in my store. My job was to talk with him, understand what he was looking for, and help him to feel fantastic in whatever he tried on. What you're selling has a longer sales cycle. You have to understand the perspective of the person you are talking to, figure out what he knows, and how he might help you get closer to the decision maker."

Bill continued, "I did not wake up this morning looking to solve Wayne's future training problems. However, Wayne may have awakened this morning thinking about his training problems. Or, more likely, Wayne's store manager has been thinking about their employee training problems because those are his daily headaches. Am I your buyer? No. But I likely know someone who is. So, if I were you, I would want to know the answer to two questions." Bill held up his two pointer fingers.

"First, who would most benefit from solving human resource type problems in this company? Second, what is the greatest benefit from that person's perspective? As JD says, 'You can't get what you want until they get what they want.'"

Mackenzie nodded along with what Bill was saying. In her excitement of the idea, she had forgotten some of the rules.

Bill continued, "And if you want to eventually make this sale, you need to figure out what kind of outcome you'd like from me or my favorable access. However, you need to direct me in order for this to be a productive introduction."

"You're right. I'm sorry, I did get ahead of myself,"

Mackenzie apologized, realizing her error. "Today I didn't even think Wayne's stores would be a prospect or even a suspect. This idea just popped into my head as you were talking."

"I get that," Bill offered. "However, thoughts need to simmer in your mind before telling them to a potential prospect. Salespeople who 'act on their feet' have had a lot of practice, and they know timing is important. Also, how you frame your question is important. JD is the expert on the sale of non-tangible goods. He hasn't told you about alignment opportunities, has he?"

OWN YOUR DIRECTION
Chapter 31

Mackenzie shook her head letting Bill know she had not heard of alignment opportunities. JD had mentioned the term, alignment, and it seemed self-explanatory, but she didn't know how framing questions would help with alignment.

Bill responded, "JD picked up on a few scenarios in my stories where I used alignment questions, often in an 'If-then' format. He tweaked those statements and started trying them on his own. JD now has a way of prompting his clients to imagine scenarios and to work together towards a common vision. He calls this 'alignment.'"

Bill paused to think then added, "I'll tell you what. If there were a way that you can get JD to teach you about alignment, then I'll set up a meeting for you and Wayne for next Friday. Are you interested in that?"

Mackenzie nodded enthusiastically, "Bill that would be incredible. Yes."

Bill responded, "I like the direction you were heading, Mackenzie. I vaguely recall Wayne grumbling about how his store managers complain about this next generation not knowing the basics of customer service and having to start from square one. I'll speak with Wayne this week. It will be on you to deliver."

Mackenzie's heart leaped. *A potential prospect!* And then she tensed up, worried that she wouldn't be able to get JD's time before the meeting with Wayne. She sensed an opportunity with Bill's favorable access, "Bill, may I ask you a favor?"

"Certainly," Bill responded.

"I don't have JD's contact info; I've just sought him out at every bike ride. Could you please give him a call now and put him on speaker?"

"Sure," he tapped on his phone to make the call.

Just as it rang for the fourth time, JD picked up. "Hey Coach, what are you up to?"

Bill signaled to Mackenzie to talk. "Hi, JD, this is Mackenzie. I'm here talking with Bill, and I asked him to call you. Is there any chance we can talk for a few minutes on Monday morning at the coffee shop?"

"Oh, hi, Mackenzie. What is it that you want to talk about?" JD asked.

"Bill said that if I can learn about alignment from you, he'll set up a meeting with Wayne for me. My CEO is coming into the office on Monday, and I'm also hoping you could give me some advice on how to create more favorable access."

"Got it. Hmmm. Okay, I've got Monday morning 5:30 to 6 AM blocked off for you. I'll meet you at Dynamo Coffee."

"Thank you, JD. I really appreciate your help."

"You're welcome. And Bill? I saw Tyrone yesterday looking for trouble. I told him to go to see you next week. Let me know if he follows through."

"Will do," Bill replied.

As Bill hit the icon to end the call, he looked at Mackenzie and asked, "So what's your CEO doing in town?"

Mackenzie sighed, "I'm not sure if it's a routine visit to the branch office or if he is going to fire all of us like my manager keeps threatening. I'm pretty sure he's going to insist on some kind of change in our sales team. I'm a little nervous, to be honest."

Bill leaned forward and asked, "Mackenzie, what does it mean when a car has its turn signal on?"

She opened her mouth to respond with the obvious answer when Bill barked, "Nothing! It means absolutely nothing!" Bill leaned back in his seat, relaxed, "All I know for certain is that the turn signal is on. I'm not certain that the car is going to turn. There are a few things in life we can be certain of, and change is one of them."

Bill shifted forward in his seat again, "I've given hundreds of speeches in my life and talked with thousands of people. Most of us fear change. But we have to realize that there's no such thing as staying the same; we are always changing each season. As individuals, we are working to make ourselves better, or we are allowing ourselves to get worse. Even in small ways, we must look for better ways."

Mackenzie thought about how Stan wanted the crew to run through the numbers and not to ask any questions. He wasn't looking for better ways to do things. He didn't know about the Steps & Rules. If Mackenzie wanted to follow JD's advice, she'd have to risk not being liked by her boss and maybe even be fired because she wasn't conforming to his standards.

Bill continued, "Instead of looking for his gain in every situation, JD turns it around and looks for someone else's gain. He knows that when people feel good around him, good things happen, and he's able to celebrate someone else's gain. That's not to say that things always go as planned. They don't.

"JD has been in a lot of tough situations, which is why, over the years, he has learned where to draw boundaries. In his early twenties, he thought every outcome was up to him, including other people's success in life. People had helped him, so he was going to help other people. He started to open doors for others, setting up others for success. But then he took it a few steps too far. He began to also carry their problems, their failures, their burdens, their issues. He carried more and more of their weight, thinking that he was helping them to heal.

"What he found was that they became dependent on him, and then they started to feel entitled to his help. They expected him to be there for them at every call, every need. He's human. He started to burn out. He was exhausted. He can't be anyone's everything. He's not made to carry someone else's burdens forever. The only one up to that job is God."

Bill paused. "JD learned that he was not capable of being anyone's everything. He learned that the people he was helping needed to own their decisions, both successes and failures. Failing, in a curious way, is winning. You can win from failing when you take responsibility for your failure and use the lesson as motivation to succeed in the next venture.

"When others did fail, he had their backs. He supported them long enough to catch their breath, gave them advice, gave them a push in the right direction, and sometimes introduced them to someone who could offer another perspective. He stopped carrying their weight and instead started to ride beside them for a short time.

"He shows others, by example, that they can succeed, but they have to find their own reasons to push themselves toward success, just like Frank did. Frank had failed in reading, but that didn't mean that he was a failure. We set up a paceline for him and gave him a push in the right direction. He felt the pull of the draft, and he decided to start training harder on his own."

Mackenzie nodded. That was exactly what JD had done for her. She realized that Bill was gently letting her know that she should not depend on JD being one call away. She wasn't meant to lean on JD or Bill to solve her problems or calm her fears; instead, she needed to take what she was learning and own her direction and practice on her own skills. She needed a paceline team to help her along the way, but she had to train on her own. This was Bill's way of cautioning her to set her expectations accordingly. "Bill, thank you for saying this. It's hard not to lean on someone who offers his wisdom and who has succeeded on the same roads. Yet, ultimately, I make the choices to determine my direction, and I need to own that. Thank you."

"You're welcome, Mackenzie. You have a bright future ahead of you, I can tell. You're willing to learn from your failures, take advice, and take a different line. That will serve you well in your many years ahead. I look forward to hearing about your meeting with Wayne."

"Bill, thank you," she rose to shake his hand confidently and smiled.

CREATING ALIGNMENT
Chapter 32

JD and Mackenzie sat across from each other on Monday morning at Dynamo Coffee. JD started the discussion with his thoughts, "There seemed to be some urgency with your call. You also said that Bill would be introducing you to Wayne this week, correct?"

Mackenzie nodded.

"Tell me why you think Bill wanted you to learn about alignment," JD stated.

Mackenzie answered, "I was thinking about that. I had never considered Bill or the clothing stores to be a customer. But as Bill was talking, I realized that he can communicate the kind of stories that get people engaged, which is what my product showcases best. So I told him that and asked what he thought about it."

"Ah," JD acknowledged.

Mackenzie didn't understand JD's reply; clearly, there was something he was thinking about. She had a feeling that he was about to tell her his thoughts.

JD continued, "Step 6 is: Create alignment. Identify the problem and align what they need with what you can do for them.

STEP 6: *Create alignment. Identify the problem and align what they need with what you can do for them.*

"Alignment is about capturing the customer's needs and presenting it back to them as a way for you to paint the picture of what it is that they want. This is a powerful tool in selling a complex product. I'm not sure you were yet at the point to use alignment, but it sounds like you were close.

"When you asked Bill what he thought about your idea, you were being lazy; you didn't take the time to set anything up for him to visualize. You only threw out an idea that he hadn't thought about before. He hadn't stated that he wanted his stories captured. That was your idea. In order to set up alignment, you have to ask your customer enough questions to get him to state what it is that he wants or needs. Your job is to know what your product can or cannot do and align the customer's needs with your product's capabilities."

JD paused. "Before we dig deeper into alignment, I'd like to ask you: How do you sell your product?"

Mackenzie was expecting only to take notes, not to be asked any questions. She was taken off guard but recovered quickly by bouncing the question, "JD, that's a great question. Are you asking that because you want to know the best aspects of my product or if I actually believe in what I'm selling?"

JD nodded. "Good bounce. I want to know if you believe in what you're selling and if so, why you do."

"Sounds good. I believe in my product because it's simple, it's personalized, it's versatile, and you can deploy it anywhere. Most safety training and employee onboarding programs have you tied to your computer, and the content is outdated and boring. I've talked with Safety Directors who have told me about lives being saved with our safety training; I've heard from HR Directors who have told me about how their employees are more excited about work because they are reminded about the bigger picture with their personalized content.

"Our product works best when the client company believes in their product as much as we believe in ours. OnboardMobile is only as good as its content. We have a library of standard content, but what makes us different and better is how we are able to assist the leaders' companies and teams in developing two minute videos and distributing the message internally. We're able to catch 'best practices' from their internal practice leaders. Then, what makes us unique is our testing. We don't want employees just to watch the video and forget it; we make sure that the lesson sticks. We do this with proprietary testing methods that really make the person think about the answers so that it sticks in their longer term memory."

JD nodded his head, "Nice. Now, I want you to translate what you just said into a sales meeting with a customer. Let's have that customer be me, as the owner of this Dynamo coffee chain."

Mackenzie asked, "Am I pretending that I know what I know about you or am I acting like this is my first meeting with you?"

JD responded, "Pretend like you have strong favorable access with a mutual connection which is how you were introduced to me. Remember that you don't yet have direct favorable access, so it is extremely important to keep the Rules top of mind. And, as always, before the meeting, set the agenda and email it to set the expectations."

Mackenzie, "Right. The agenda. History first." She paused and leaned forward, pretending that she was beginning the actual meeting, developing rapport, "JD, I've heard from a number of people that you have an ability to get to know the

CREATING ALIGNMENT 169

core of people rather quickly. So, I don't think it's a stretch to assume that you've hired excellent store managers?"

JD nodded affirmatively.

Mackenzie continued, "Even with excellent store managers, it can be difficult to manage across multiple stores. Tell me about the history of your employee hiring and training process."

JD interrupted, "Hold on. I'm going to stop you there. Remember, you are talking with the owner. Is the owner of a multi-store coffee shop doing the new employee hiring?" JD paused as Mackenzie shook her head. "Likely not. It's important to approach the prospect from his or her perspective."

"Okay, so let me try that again," Mackenzie took a deep breath. "JD, even with excellent store managers, it can be difficult to manage across stores. How have you handled your new employee hiring and training?"

"Better," JD nodded. "Well, Mackenzie, it's usually the store managers who are doing the new employee hiring and training. I just provide the training overview for them. I try to stay out of the details as much as possible and work more on strategy, but I make sure they know what my standards are."

"Could you tell me about how your store managers decide which training tools to use and how you deliver your message?" Mackenzie inquired.

JD nodded again, "Good start. There is a high likelihood that the store manager is too busy to properly train and explain the standards. Now, I want to pause again and explain a few things. With every meeting, as you know, your main goal is to develop trust with your contact. In building trust with an executive, you need to realize that different execs have different priorities, but growing revenue profitably is almost always near the top. The executive is responsible for the bottom line and needs to have the business make money in order to stay in business.

"As you know, profit is the difference between the income and the amount spent in buying, operating, or producing something. So that's money coming in from sales, minus the product costs, employee expenses, rent, insurance, and other business costs. Then, there is the cost of buying your product, which isn't essential to your prospect unless you paint the picture that it is essential.

"As a salesperson, there are certain aspects of profit that you may know. You know about the effects of direct costs on profit. Additionally, from what you spoke about earlier, it seems you are focusing on the indirect cost of employees' engagement, where higher engagement equals a more productive workforce. Then you talked about safety, so you're aware of the indirect price tag of having an injured worker.

"Often the full spectrum of these costs is hard to measure. Do you know the difference between price and cost from the perspective of your customer?" JD asked.

"STEPS" OF THE SALES PROCESS

Step 1: Understand your general access.
Step 2: Develop a plan to gain favorable access.
Step 3: Leverage favorable access to get a meeting.
Step 4: Set the agenda and then put the customer in control.
Step 5: Build trust through dialogue.
Step 6: <u>Create alignment. Identify the problem and align what they need with what you can do for them.</u>

"RULES" OF THE PACELINE

Rule 1: You can't get what you want until they get what they want.
Rule 2: Go slow to go fast.
Rule 3: Questions are rarely questions. Understand the why.
Rule 4: Make significant deposits before withdrawing or asking for a loan.
Rule 5: Practice until the process becomes instinctive.
Rule 6: Communicate the value of your vision in their terms.
Rule 7: Provide perspective not just content.
Rule 8: People don't care how much you know until they know how much you care.

MEASURING COST
Chapter 33

Mackenzie nodded, "I may have an idea of the difference between cost and price for my customer, but I think your answer would be better. Please go on."

JD didn't hesitate, "A powerful question to ask yourself and your customers is: What is the true cost of not having safety, Risk Control, or proper onboarding of employees? Most owners and managers do not fully understand the factors that play into the true cost.

"People do understand the price tag of something and to them it can feel expensive or inexpensive according to the value they attribute to your product. According to your customers, their total cost equals price minus the value. The value to the customer determines the ultimate cost to the customer. The higher the value that your customer puts on your product, the lower the cost is to them. Your customer will find a way to afford the price because the value is much greater to them."

Mackenzie could see how his quasi-equation would work. She had certainly valued something so highly that even if she couldn't budget for it, she figured out a way to get it.

JD continued, "And there's a second piece to distinguishing between cost and price which is called variation. When you have 'low variation' with your product, you get 'higher quality,' which equals 'lower cost.' The opposite is also true: 'high variation' with your product produces 'lower quality' and results in 'higher cost.'

JD took out a pen and drew on a napkin as he summarized, "These aren't rules, they are just good to keep top of mind when you are talking to prospects. Cost = Price - Value; Low Variation = High Quality = Low Cost."

JD pushed the napkin across the table to Mackenzie and transitioned, "Let's go back to this coffee shop. What is Dynamo selling? And I do want to hear your answer."

"Coffee, obviously," Mackenzie stated.

"Nope," JD shook his head.

Mackenzie looked confused.

"If someone just wanted a coffee, they would go buy the lowest priced coffee or make their own. Why would anyone pay over three dollars for a cup of coffee? There's something else bringing them here. Try again," JD prompted.

"Convenience?" Mackenzie ventured. JD wasn't impressed. Mackenzie then offered, "Or maybe they like coming into the shop?"

JD nodded. "Yes. It's the experience. This coffee shop is selling a valuable experience. Now, when you have high quality training of baristas, you get lower variation between two different baristas serving your customers. When your customer service variation is low across different baristas, you receive an overall higher quality customer experience. This equates to lowering your cost per customer because your customers value their high quality experience and will return.

"Now, what happens when you lose your best baristas frequently?" JD asked.

Mackenzie remained silent. JD was on a roll.

"Your variation of the customer experience gets higher, which makes the customer's quality of experience lower, which increases the cost of your product. Let's add that to the equation of what it costs to replace an employee.

"This is why employee turnover costs more than most people think it does. Depending on the job, this can vary from a few thousand dollars, on the low end, to tens of thousands of dollars on the high end. Here in this coffee shop, replacing a barista will likely cost the store around two to five thousand dollars, if you factor in the hours recruiting, training, and bringing a new barista up to speed. That's not even contemplating the cost to the customer experience as the lost employee causes higher variation in the product or service.

"How many cups of coffee does the owner need to sell to cover the loss of his employee? If the store makes one dollar per cup of coffee and it cost three thousand dollars to replace an employee, that's three thousand more cups of coffee to break even! Most people don't understand the indirect factors of this cost. Let me give you examples from my world of expertise that most people don't know about: insurance."

DIGGING DEEPER
Chapter 34

Mackenzie had read about JD's career path. He had started as an intern at some kind of insurance agency and worked his way up the ladder over the next ten years to become the President and CEO, a position he held for a decade. Mackenzie didn't know much about insurance, except that she had to enroll and purchase health insurance when she was hired at OnBoardMobile. The company had two options for her online, so she didn't understand how JD could become the greatest salesperson by selling insurance. She figured that he was selling a more complicated kind of insurance which must have taken more expertise.

JD continued, "Worker's Compensation is a type of insurance that most states require business owners to purchase in order to cover injuries of their employees on the job. In determining the insurance premium, or price, of Worker's Comp, insurance companies use a factor called an 'Experience Modification.' In the industry, we call the Experience Modification the 'ex-mod.' If the frequency and severity of injuries are equal to the average for your industry, your ex-mod is 1.00. If the frequency and severity of injuries are more than average, your ex-mod is over 1.00. This factor is a big indicator of your insurance premium. Your basic rates are multiplied by your ex-mod. Anything more than 1.00 and you will likely be paying more for your insurance coverage than your competitors.

"From what I've seen, ex-mods of more than 1.00 usually happen with untrained and disgruntled employees. The more they dislike their jobs, the more likely they'll have lower production and be careless about what they are doing. This leads to greater probability of them getting injured and taking longer to return to work.

"I often worked with the CFO on insurance matters, and the CFO would always direct me to lower their direct insurance premium price. I would instead ask the CFO for their ex-mod and the details to their Worker's Comp injuries. When their ex-mod was above 1.00, I'd look for trends in their workers' injuries. And then I would ask, 'What is your employee turnover? And, how much does it cost for you to replace a worker?' If they didn't know these numbers, then I knew that they had a problem. I would also ask about the details of their company culture and how they communicated their company message to the employees. These were questions that they had never heard from an insurance broker.

"The point of all the questions was to get them to realize that there is usually more to the picture than just the price of their Worker's Comp insurance. It was possible that the Worker's Comp insurance carrier would reduce their premiums; I could usually get a 10% decrease in new business. On a $50,000 premium, that's $5,000 back into the CFO's budget, which makes the CFO look good. But how much more could I bring back to their budget if we worked on their employee turnover? When we get to the root of the problem, we could bring hundreds of thousands of dollars back to their bottom line. How does the CFO look with those numbers?"

Like a star, Mackenzie acknowledged silently.

ALWAYS LEARNING, ALWAYS GROWING
Chapter 35

JD looked around, "Let's consider this coffee shop. Why does the Dynamo cycling group meet at this particular location?"

Mackenzie responded, "I did wonder about that. At first, I thought it was a convenient location. But, from what I have learned, the owner used to be a cyclist, and he knew someone in the group and started catering to the riders."

"You're right. It's not the location. There are other coffee shops which are more convenient for our regular rides. It's favorable access that opened the door, and it's the demand-pull that the owner created in the experience that makes people come back. He hosted the group rides and offered beer on Friday nights to provide a place for the riders to hang out.

"He made internal investments to polish their customer service. Notice how they call the regular customers by name. Look at how clean this shop is. Notice how they dress comfortably, yet professionally. Notice how the coffee is just the way you like it, every time. That's not by accident. The owner has invested in the employees, and in return, most of these employees have been here for over two years and many have moved up. He understands that Low Variation = High Quality = Low Cost. The owner is now working with a few of his longer-term employees to figure out when and where they could open new Dynamo Coffee Shops in other cities."

"How do you know all of that?" Mackenzie blurted.

JD cracked a wry smile.

"Okay, I know how you know all that. Clearly, the Steps. But why do you care about knowing all of that?" she asked.

"Mackenzie, I'm always learning, always growing. I challenge myself to fuel my curiosity. I'm interested in finding out if the Steps are applicable to all businesses. Are they basic and general enough to apply anywhere, and are they specific enough to make a difference? It's fun for me to keep testing them. I stay curious with every conversation with the purpose to test the sales process, which is how I came up with the alignment questions.

"Now, take what you've just learned about this coffee shop owner and apply it. I'm the coffee shop owner again, and you want to sell me your product. Go."

Mackenzie felt like she was being tested in a job interview. Her heart rate rose. That was an overwhelming amount of information, and she didn't know where to start. *Calm down. This is practice. Start with the owner.* "Okay. I'm impressed with how much you invest into your managers, JD. You must spend a lot of time with them! How do you have time to train your managers and keep the business running smoothly?"

"That's a great question. I work late and wake up early to get things done. I've also asked a few of my long-term managers to take on some ownership responsibilities. I like to make the main decisions, but I know I have to delegate some things if I ever want to establish more stores in different cities."

"I hear you. It's hard to let things go because we know exactly how we want things done. It takes time to eventually make time. It seems like the employee handbooks take a lot of time to complete with all of the regulatory requirements of job descriptions, detailing sanitary conditions, external requirements like HIPPA, Cobra, FMLA, sexual harassment, enrollment, and eligibility, to name a few, and those topics are not even discussing the job training. Do you have a training manual that you use?" Mackenzie asked as she tried to think of the next question.

"We have an old one but it is so out of date that I'm sure we're out of compliance now. I spent so much time with my first managers, walking them through everything. It took a long time for us to get that first manual written. We had a rocky start and almost went under because I had higher standards than my managers could deliver with limited practice. Our customers were frustrated. Managers quit. Baristas quit. Thankfully, a few of my managers and baristas stuck with me, and we made it work."

Mackenzie asked, "How many new employees do your managers train every year?" Mackenzie knew this was a softball question, but it was the first question that came to her mind.

"In the last two years, it's only been a handful of employees. But, we're thinking about opening Dynamo Coffee Shops in a few new cities next year, if things work out as we've planned."

"Have you ever thought about moving your manager and employee training to a mobile video format?" she asked, hoping this was a good question to lead him to her product.

"Stop right there. You're moving too fast. Your early questions were good. You're gathering good info. But you don't yet have enough to introduce your product. However, you do have enough info to let your prospect know that this conversation is going somewhere and that you're listening. You know that your prospect doesn't have enough time in his day to do the kind of training he wants. You know that he thinks his training manual is obsolete. You also know that your prospect has a particular way he likes to talk, express, and bring his personality into his work. So this is where you can bring in your first if-then alignment question. It might be something like this:

"If there were a way for you to create fresh training content and speed up the delivery of your training process while keeping your signature touch on the training, then would that be of interest to you?"

That is a powerful question, Mackenzie thought.

JD continued, "You already know the answer to this because your prospect has already stated exactly what you presented. This is a soft way of affirming what your prospect already wants, and you know that your product can provide the solution. It's a win-win. Let's switch roles right now. You be the owner, I'll be the salesperson.

"If there were a way for you to create fresh training content and speed up the delivery of your training process while keeping your signature touch on the training, then would that be of interest to you?" JD repeated.

"Of course," Mackenzie replied.

"Okay, well in order to do that, may I ask you a few more questions?" he asked.

Mackenzie nodded.

"Are you satisfied with the outcome of your store manager hiring and training new employees?"

Mackenzie answered with her first thought, "She does an excellent job hiring and training the details."

"Is she able to communicate with the same passion for why you do things the way that you do?" JD probed further.

"Probably not," Mackenzie responded, unsure of how JD wanted her to answer.

"If there were a way to combine her hands-on expertise with your passion for the company, then would that be of interest to you?"

"Sure!" Mackenzie was seeing where he was going.

"Great. In order to do that, may I ask you a few more questions?"

"Yes," Mackenzie nodded, feeling the excitement of the conversation.

GAINING A DIFFERENT PERSPECTIVE
Chapter 36

JD placed both hands on the table, "Okay, we'll stop here again. Do you notice how my questions are helping you to be open to new questions? Instead of being defensive, did you feel how your attitude changed to be interested in what's possible? I haven't mentioned my product at all. I'm not selling. I'm just trying to understand the customer's needs and values and then I'm re-framing what is said into a possibility. Does that make sense?"

"Yes, but I don't know if I could think of all those questions on the fly. How do you do that so smoothly?" Mackenzie asked.

"Rule 5: Practice until the process becomes instinctive. When your process becomes instinctive, you're able to fully focus on the person in front of you and be able to uncover what he says between the lines. This will require lots of excellent practice, especially of Rule 3: Questions are rarely questions. When your customer asks you a question, you'll be able to bounce the question to understand why the question was asked.

"You will make mistakes, and you will ask dead-end questions, especially in your learning years. Some prospects will blast you after your dead-end questions. Know that it's normal and admit that you asked a poor question. Re-state it. Say, 'let me ask that a different way' or 'please let me back up. I want to understand your perspective, and I appreciate your patience with me.' If it starts to go badly, re-state what your prospect has said so you can re-group."

"Okay," Mackenzie said as she took an audible breath.

"Mackenzie, learning how to create demand-pull takes time. It's not automatic. This is why Rule 5, excellent practice, is so important. You have to practice and refine your practice; you have to look for ways to improve your practice. By practicing the techniques of the Steps & Rules, you'll be years ahead of churn-and-burn cold-calling salespeople who go straight for the sale and quickly move on to the next target. Those churn-and-burn salespeople can rise fast but they also burn out fast, and they burn out their prospects with their techniques."

Mackenzie nodded. She had been jealous of her bulldog colleague, Jack, who closed a few deals quickly after he was hired. But after asking Tommy a few questions in the last week, she learned that Jack had previous connections to his initial customers. Even though Jack didn't know the term favorable access, he had used his favorable access and then pushed his sales through the process quickly. She had also learned that Jack had been grumbling about his customers calling him with complaints and that he was starting to blame OnBoard's customer service for his problems. There was more to the story, but the superficial view was showing Mackenzie that Jack's fast rise might be more of a churn-and-burn technique that she should not try to mimic. In her mind, she agreed that the Steps & Rules were worth practicing.

JD continued, "And know that in your business, it will take multiple meetings for you to gather the information you need to bring value and build trust. There is a big difference in approaching the client as a salesperson looking to make the fast sale versus a salesperson looking to provide value as a consultant. Depending on the customer, it may make sense for you to ask if you can shadow their business for a day. We did this a lot in our business. You'll know more of what it's like to be in a prospect's shoes when you walk briefly in their shoes.

"After you see some of their processes, resist the desire to fix any problems you see. Instead, ask more questions to understand why they do what they do. For instance, if you notice the baristas tossing excess milk away, instead of pointing that out to the owner, ask the barista why he does that. There may be a logical reason for it. A day walking in someone else's shoes does not make you the expert. Instead, it just gives you a different perspective and the ability to ask better questions.

"That being said, there are a few things I've learned over the decades that are hot button topics, especially with Human Resources/ Employee Engagement/ Whatever-they're-calling-it-these-days. Depending on the size of the company, the HR manager recruits, presents the compensation package, explains the 401k, enrolls new hires into the benefit packages, handles compliance issues, insurance, injuries on the job, and wrongful termination litigation, as well as trains new hires. Which responsibility do you think slides to the bottom of the list?"

Mackenzie stayed silent and let him continue.

"You'll find out when you have someone walk you through their training schedule and ask when those sessions get scheduled. Depending on workflow and company resources, the training often gets the lowest priority. The company may have each new employee run through a paper manual or boring digital content with obvious answers, just to check the compliance box to avoid getting fined by regulators or sued for negligence. Most likely the training stops there, and the rest is on-the-job training."

Mackenzie didn't understand the difference between the two. She had always thought they were the same thing.

JD explained, "There's a big difference between on-the-job-training and training-on-the-job. The former is: jump in and swim or drown. I've seen a lot of injuries in physical jobs and a lot of turnover in sedentary on-the-job training. Training-on-the-job is intentionality of training. New hires are paired with seasoned employees who have the enthusiasm and ability to teach. Most companies do not have seasoned employees with enthusiasm, ability, and capacity in their day to teach. Who has time to do all of that? This is where I see your product having an impact."

JD paused to gather his thoughts. "If there were a way for your company to leverage and multiply the time of your internal leaders to train in a way that reduces confusion, reduces injury, and increases engagement by delivering your culture and values in a personal way, then would you be interested in hearing more about how we could make that happen?"

Mackenzie reacted with delight, "That's really good, JD. Hold on, I need to write that down."

JD didn't wait. He kept going, "Alignment questions are extremely important. You align what they say with what is possible. That's what makes them so powerful."

COMMUNICATING VALUE
Chapter 37

JD continued, "And now we arrive at Step 7: Control the question and direction.

STEP 7: *Control the question and the direction.*

What I like to say here is, 'In order to see if we can do X, Y, and Z, I need to ask you a few more questions.' This is when you start getting insight into who to talk with next. You ask, 'Is there someone else who needs to have buy-in on this vision?' This question is necessary for setting up your next meeting. Or you can wait on this step as you may need to find out if you can implement the vision that your prospect has created.

"In this scenario at our coffee shop, depending on your prospect's attitude toward training, you would ask him a leading question. If training is a drain to him, ask him something like: 'If you didn't have to deliver training to new managers, would that increase your capacity to do the other important operations?'

"The answer is obvious. You follow up with a more open-ended question: So if we could increase your inventory of time what value would that be to you?

"On the other hand, if training excites him, you might ask: If you could redesign your training curriculum, could you see it helping your culture and improving your operations? And follow up with, 'Tell me more about that' and 'what else do you need from me in order to make this happen?'

"Then after all of the meetings walking through these steps, discovering their needs, you arrive at Step 8: Summarize and guide with next steps.

***STEP 8**: Summarize and guide with next steps.*

"Summarize what you've heard and set up the following meeting for what you need to do next. If you need to talk with another decision maker, then ask for the introduction from the person in your current meeting.

"The conclusion of the Steps is to repeat all of the Steps again! With every new relationship in the prospect's company, no matter if you've received a warm or cold referral—you start back with Step 1 to 2, 3, 4, and 5: Move from general access to favorable access, favorable access to a meeting, set the agenda, then use the meeting to build trust.

"In subsequent meetings, usually at the proposal stage, you end by reading the agenda, making sure everything was covered to their satisfaction and ending with open-ended questions. One suggestion: 'Do you see the value of OnBoardMobile improving your onboarding and your message of the values and standards you have for your company and employee culture?'

"You're doing this to custom-create a product based on your prospects' needs. It's the same product you've always been selling, but the difference is that you are communicating how their needs matter and how your specific product can help solve their particular problem."

JD sat back in his chair and said, "And those are the Steps of the sales process cycle. Now, depending on the business, the owner or CEO may delegate detailed decisions to other managers or C-level execs. You'll want to find out that information and ask for the referral to talk with that contact. Build your paceline. The same steps apply. 'If there were a way to ask a few questions of your store manager to make sure I get a full picture and better understand training perspectives and circle back to confirm that information with you, then would that be of interest to you?'"

JD switched and began to play the role of the client, "'You're going to help me create capacity in my business? Yes and absolutely!'

"When you start using alignment, it will feel contrived. But to the other person, they are being affirmed and told that what they say really does matter."

JD leaned forward again, "That was a lot of information at once, I know. Usually we handle that over a few meetings, but I think you're ready to get the full picture now, test it out, fumble, and practice again. Rule 5 in action. Is that fair?"

Mackenzie nodded. "Thank you for covering all of that material, JD. Yes, it's time to practice until the process becomes instinctive."

8 "STEPS" OF THE SALES PROCESS

Step 1: Understand your general access.
Step 2: Develop a plan to gain favorable access.
Step 3: Leverage favorable access to get a meeting.
Step 4: Set the agenda and then put the customer in control.
Step 5: Build trust through dialogue.
Step 6: Create alignment. Identify the problem and align what they need with what you can do for them.
Step 7: Control the question and the direction.
Step 8: Summarize and guide with next steps.

8 "RULES" OF THE PACELINE

Rule 1: You can't get what you want until they get what they want.
Rule 2: Go slow to go fast.
Rule 3: Questions are rarely questions. Understand the why.
Rule 4: Make significant deposits before withdrawing or asking for a loan.
Rule 5: Practice until the process becomes instinctive.
Rule 6: Communicate the value of your vision in their terms.
Rule 7: Provide perspective not just content.
Rule 8: People don't care how much you know until they know how much you care.

PART FOUR

Simple Solutions

> # TIMING
> ## Chapter 38

Mackenzie paused, wondering if this was the right time to transition to her secondary reason for meeting with JD. She needed a stronger paceline at work. It didn't appear that her manager, Stan, would be interested in helping her via a paceline, but she wanted to try asking for her CEO's help. She knew she didn't have much time with JD, so she continued, "And my first chance to practice it will be tomorrow with my CEO."

JD's expression appeared to disagree with her, but he didn't respond to her statement. He instead asked a question, "What questions did you have in mind to ask me about the perspective of the CEO?"

Mackenzie replied, "Well, I wanted to ask you about favorable access through another person. How will I know when it is okay to ask another person to introduce me to someone in their circle of favorable access?"

"Interesting question. Tell me why you are asking it," JD stated.

"Well," Mackenzie started, "Stan, my sales manager, shut that door in my face. Likely I was too fast in asking and messed that up, but I have another chance at a meeting with my CEO tomorrow; he's coming in to talk presumably about sales. Stan and my CEO have very similar social circles, and I think that's because my CEO was involved in just about every community board when he used to live here. It seems risky to ask the CEO for introductions. If he says 'no' like Stan, then I will likely offend both the CEO and my manager, right?"

"Yes, that is risky and likely premature to ask for that. You have to build trust with Rules 1 through 4 first. If you are successful at doing that, the answer is that it all depends on your CEO's perspective. Did your CEO ever spend time as a salesperson? Does he know what it's like to make dead-end sales calls? What was his first sale and how did he get it? Does he remember his first sale as being solely through his own hard work or does he realize that someone else opened the door for him? If he acknowledges that his job is to open doors and make it easier for his salespeople to sell, then he's likely someone to ask after you've made a few deposits and developed direct favorable access. However, if you find that he's of the same mindset as Stan, then you're on your own, and you'll have to find someone else to help you."

"That's good advice. Thank you, JD," Mackenzie said earnestly. She realized that she had pushed too quickly with Karen and Stan, which ended in failure. She didn't want to make the same mistake with her CEO, so she decided the best way to find out her CEO's perspective would be to listen well and to ask a few good questions during his visit to the office.

PODIUM STAND
Chapter 39

JD stood up to shake her hand, signaling their time was complete. But then he interjected, "Oh, one more thing. Do you have a goal with your cycling?"

Mackenzie thought about his question and Rule 3 popped in her head, "JD, that's an interesting question, why do you ask?"

JD gave her a thumbs up, "Perfectly bounced, Mackenzie. There's a race coming up. I think you should challenge yourself and enter the race. You may surprise yourself."

"I hadn't thought about that. I'll look into signing up." Mackenzie looked at her watch, 5:55 AM; she was nearing her time limit and knew to respect his time. She stood with him and said, "JD, I can't thank you enough for your time and wisdom. I've thought about a few different ways to thank you, but they don't seem to fit. You probably don't like gifts, and you probably aren't looking for dinner or to be taken to a sports event. From what you've said before, you seem like the type of person who wants to know that your words and effort made a difference in someone else's life. And you've made a huge difference in my life. But besides just telling you, how else can I thank you?"

JD laughed, "Mackenzie, I like how direct you are in trying to figure out the answer to Rule 1. You're right; I don't like gifts, I get antsy watching an entire game at a stadium, and I don't want to go to dinner.

"That being said, gifts are usually the easiest thank you because it takes zero time out of the recipient's day and even if the gift is off the mark, it is usually a nice gesture. Sports events and dinners usually happen in the evenings, and I am very selective on how I spend my evenings. My wife and I have an agreement that dinner meetings are to be limited unless it's a unique investment opportunity, a board meeting engagement, or it's a dinner that she wants to attend. Additionally, I wake up at 4:30 AM most mornings; I cannot do that if I'm out late."

JD hesitated and sat back down. Mackenzie re-seated herself as well. JD continued, "And I usually do not tell people this, but you may not hear this elsewhere. What I'm about to say next may seem unfair to you. And it is, but it is the way it is because we live in a fallen world." JD paused again, clearly thinking about how to phrase what he was going to say next.

"For you, as a young woman early in your sales career, it's difficult to set boundaries. Sales are all about relationship building, and you do have to be careful with whom and how you build your relationships. You have to decide if extra protection of your character, perceived or otherwise, is worth the inconvenience. I've seen too many business women and men fail to set boundaries for themselves because they think they can handle whatever comes their way. Especially when alcohol is added to the picture, they lose perspective of what they thought they could handle. In the long run, it's better to stay above the fray and to set boundaries early in your career.

"In the sales world, there's a lot of wine-ing and dining, and you'll have to get creative in order to set boundaries. It will mean you'll miss out on a few opportunities. It will also mean that you'll know where you draw the line and you won't get caught up in back-door politics. Setting those boundaries has been one of the most important reasons I'm still happily married. Trust takes years to build and only one moment to break.

"One other important lesson I've learned is to treat loved ones as well as you treat your customers. This is so much easier to say than to actually live out in our day to day lives. In sales, we get paid for our ability to build relationships. It's very difficult to keep up the same energy at home that we give to our prospects in business. Sales meetings and opportunities are relatively quick time spans where you have to be 'on.' Anyone can be charming for a limited amount of time. In a long-lasting family relationship, quick charm doesn't give what your family needs or wants, and it doesn't get you what you want. In order to have the energy to give to my wife and kids, I have to say 'no' to situations that will ultimately erode my family's time and trust. If you don't stand for anything, you'll fall for everything."

Mackenzie nodded. So many thoughts were swirling through her head, but she was too shocked by his candor to drum up a question.

JD started again, "Back to your great question of what to give. The greatest gift you can give me is to teach another young woman what you've learned. I see too many women competing against one another and not enough of teaming up in a paceline and pulling for one another. It is difficult for me to mentor young women like yourself, due to the boundaries I have to put in place because of the confusion around intentions being misinterpreted.

"The cycling club has given me opportunities to teach you at times that are appropriate. But that does not often happen, and I don't have the kind of time it takes to teach many other women like this. So, the best way you can thank me is to teach other young women what you've learned."

Mackenzie felt honored. "I hear you, JD. Thank you for

telling me this." Then her mind fired a thought, which made Mackenzie smile and ask, "JD, if there were a way to multiply your message and provide the appropriate space and opportunity to teach more young business women, then would that be of interest to you?"

"Ha! Mackenzie that is what I call putting what you learn into practice. Way to plant that idea. I'm intrigued. I have to run to my next meeting, but I like the way you are thinking." JD stood from his seat, "Mackenzie, best of luck with your next meetings. Go get 'em."

BREAKAWAY

Chapter 40

All ten of the sales crew packed into the conference room as they did every week. What was different was that instead of the awkward silence, 'Let's Get Ready to Rumble,' an old 90s jock jam, blasted over the conference room speakers. The video screen showed a photo of an angry tiger. Mackenzie wasn't sure what sort of message they wanted to send. *Animated and animal-like?* she wondered.

Whatever message he was about to give was certainly a departure from Stan's typical start to his sales meeting which always began with his mantra, "Begin with nothing in mind and see where you end up." The crew universally thought this was the dumbest sentence they had ever heard. They knew he was trying to get them to set goals so that they had something to reach for, but instead, they wished he would give them direction on how to make a sale. Stan would usually segue from his obscure mantra into the specifics of the numbers, numbers, numbers, and more numbers. There was never a connection from the obscure beginning to the specific sales numbers they were supposed to reach, which frustrated each person on the sales crew.

Sales Manager Stan strutted into the room, exuding a confidence that she hadn't seen before. He pressed a button to silence the music and began, "I am honored to have our company's CEO here with us today. This is a man who recruited me as a salesman and mentored me as my manager. He has held numerous roles in our company, and his success is evident. Under his leadership, OnboardMobile has grown from $1 million in sales to $8 million, and he is the visionary who knows that our industry needs to raise up the next generation of salespeople. You are the testing ground for the model he wants implemented across this company. He has personally invested his efforts into who he wanted to hire and how he wanted them trained. And he expects results. Without further ado, Mr. Tony Garcia."

The OnBoardMobile CEO smiled, "Thanks, Stan. Hi Team, it's good to meet with you today. It's true; I'm the one who wanted to bring on a group of new, fresh sales talent to use our own OnboardMobile tools in-house and in order to train up the next generation sales team into sales animals!"

So that's where he was going with the tiger? Mackenzie was expecting something more substantial from a man who was dressed flawlessly with his freshly pressed suit and tie.

"I have a vested interest in you succeeding. A few of you have really taken off with our sales training and planning. Keep knocking those doors down! However, as we all know, the majority of this crew has had trouble making progress. So, I have a question for all of you. Who wants to be successful?"

All ten of the crew raised their hands.

"What is success?" Mr. Garcia asked as he clicked to the next screen showing the words as he read, "It's the progressive realization of a worthy ideal. You have to have a worthy ideal, or goal, to move toward, and you have to keep moving toward it. We have to make progress towards the realization."

The sales crew all nodded their heads. They had all seen that quote floating around on social media before. Worthy ideals seemed like a good idea, even though they felt lofty and nebulous.

Mr. Garcia continued, "I'm going to ask you another question, and I want you to write down your answer on the corner of that sheet of paper in front of you. I want you to rip off the corner, write down your number and put it in your pocket." He paused then asked, "How much money is enough?"

Mackenzie's pen remained immobile on her torn piece of paper. The thought of writing down a random amount of money to 'be enough' made her heart sink. For her, money wasn't the end-goal. 'Do what you love and the money will follow,' was a quote that she had printed out and stuck on her fridge at home. She hoped that someday she could find fulfilling work where the money would follow.

Mr. Garcia went on, "Most of you have never thought about this. It's not that money, by itself, is important. But, you do want to make enough money so you can do the things you want to do in life."

Mackenzie did agree with his last statement. Despite her partial scholarship for track, she had significant student debt. Adding to that debt was the accumulation from additional living costs, like rent, utilities, and grocery bills; with everything piling up she felt like there was a huge headwind against her. No matter how hard she had tried to keep 'knocking those doors down' for OnBoardMobile, she just felt like she was spinning her wheels. Ironically, without a clear roadmap, she didn't understand her destination. As sincerely as Stan and Mr. Garcia had expected to win with their sales training and planning model, it was leading her nowhere. She had begun with sales goals in mind and ended up with nothing which was the flip side of Stan's less than inspirational mantra.

Mr. Garcia continued, "As a salesperson, you are essentially building your own company. We have a lucrative sales commission plan here and the only one putting a cap on your compensation is you. So build your own company within this company that allows you the freedom to do what you want to do in life. You have the freedom and the responsibility for your own outcomes."

He clicked to the next slide titled 'Goals' and said, "Every night after work, I want you to ask yourself, 'What did I do today that gets me closer to my goal?' Setting goals requires intentional striving and continuous effort to reach the ultimate objective."

Mackenzie knew goals were important, but she silently questioned how they expected her to reach her objective with their training and plan. Her mind wandered to JD and Bill's advice, and she was struck by the disconnect with what JD and Bill were teaching her and what she was currently hearing from OnBoardMobile.

Mr. Garcia pulled Mackenzie's wandering thoughts back in, "As you'll also learn, money isn't everything. So what are your larger goals with work, family, friends? That's a longer session that you can work on with Stan in the coming weeks."

A few of the sales crew exchanged glances. Stan was not someone who would be eager to talk about anything other than numbers. Mackenzie was thankful that Mr. Garcia at least acknowledged that money was not everything and that larger goals were worthy of discussion.

"As CEO, of course, I want you to believe that your work is important. Sales are everything to this company. Our company can't survive without sales. That's why I've invested in your sales team leader; I've invested in you and the process. I want you to succeed. If there's anything I can do to help you sell more of OnBoardMobile, I'm only a call away."

After all the talk about money, Mackenzie wondered if Mr. Garcia truly wanted to invest in the sales crew, or if he just wanted them to churn through call lists with the hope that his investment would bring in more money.

Mr. Garcia turned to Stan, "How are we on time? I'd like to open it up for questions."

Stan looked at his watch and said, "We have about ten minutes before we'll need to leave for our next meeting. Sure, let's take a few minutes for Q & A. Does anyone have any questions?"

Jack piped up first, "Mr. Garcia, I've talked to a number of people in this office about your legacy, and what a rich legacy it is! You put OnBoardMobile on the map here in this state with your entrepreneurial spirit. What was your background? If you can tell us one of your sales secrets, we are listening."

Mackenzie inwardly cringed at Jack's slick suck-up maneuver, but she was interested in hearing Mr. Garcia's answer.

"Well, Mr. Jack himself! I've seen your numbers, and I like what you're doing. Great question. When I was in your shoes, I was a hustler, just like you. I had a lot of people tell me 'no,' but I just marched on to the next prospect. If I struck out on one call, I just kept stepping up to the plate. Sales is hard. We strike out more than we hit a single or double. But you miss every opportunity that you don't take a swing at. We've got to keep swinging and keep our eye on the ball."

Mackenzie felt her stomach turning with all this talk about running through the numbers again. There was nothing practical, no real training. *Just keep showing up and keep swinging and maybe, if you're lucky, you'll hit one? That's all he wanted to share?* Mackenzie knew there was more; she had even read about it. *Why didn't he talk about his beginnings?* She had done her research and dug in the company's digital archives about Mr. Garcia's rise to CEO. There were a number of articles about his humble beginnings and how his hard work and a few key relationships started opening doors.

One particular article told about Garcia's first lawn business when he was 14. After he had a handful of neighborhood customers, he decided he wanted to find a way to increase his business by securing the bigger paying customers. He walked a number of miles to where the lawns were large and started observing. He knew from watching his own neighbors that when a new homeowner moved in, it usually took a number of months before they started caring about their lawn. He watched the 'for sale' signs and marked down the addresses of which homes sold and when.

He was there to greet the new homeowner and ask if he could take care of their yard. He worked meticulously, lugging his mower and edger miles after school to do the best job he could do. Over time, he got to know the homeowners, and they referred him to neighbors. He hired a few hard-working friends and taught them how to mow and edge. It was one of his loyal lawn-mowing clients who started asking him about his future and saw his potential in sales given his hands-on, hard-charging approach to work. This lawn client hired Garcia in his first salary-paid job with a new company designed to assist small businesses with outmoded technologies in their efforts to meet the new standards set by the Occupational Safety and Health Act (OSHA) of 1970.

In the article, Mr. Garcia called it a lucky break. Mackenzie saw it differently after her mentoring sessions with JD and Bill. She decided to ask it as a question. "Mr. Garcia, I read an archived article about how you started your own lawn business at 14. You said it was a lucky break to get your first salary-paying job offered from one of your lawn clients. I'm not sure that luck had anything to do with it. I think you had the foresight to position yourself with general access into the area of prestigious homes. Then you worked hard towards favorable access by making deposits and building trust in those circles. Could you tell us how you decided to knock on those front doors and how that decision led to other open doors?"

Mr. Garcia's eyes opened a little wider, and then he straightened himself. "Miss Mackenzie Jones, am I right?"

Mackenzie nodded. Her heart was pounding, and she could feel the sweat rolling down her back.

"I think you're giving me a little too much credit as a 14 year old. I was just trying to make more money and thought that bigger lawns would mean more money. It took me over a year to get my first big house client. I knocked on a lot of smaller doors before I knocked on a big one. I just kept knocking until people opened their doors. Then I worked really hard to make sure they liked the work I did for them." Mr. Garcia looked at his watch and at Stan and said, "Do we have time for one more question?"

Mackenzie's heart rate didn't slow down. Clearly, her question made Mr. Garcia uncomfortable. She would probably be canned in the next few weeks.

AERODYNAMICS
Chapter 41

Mackenzie was drowning in her thoughts and didn't even hear the last question. Everyone around her got up and started walking towards the door. She didn't notice Mr. Garcia walking directly toward her.

"Mackenzie, I haven't thought about my lawn business in a long time. I don't often refer back to my lawn-mowing days. I'd rather focus on the success I've had since then. I didn't give you a solid answer to your question because I didn't think it was relevant for this meeting."

"Mr. Garcia," Mackenzie pleaded as she stood up, "My question was too personal. This is my first sales job. You've seen my numbers. I am cutting the grass with nail clippers right now."

Mr. Garcia laughed. Mackenzie continued, "I have been knocking on doors all day, every day. But I'm realizing that this can't be just a numbers game because relationships matter. Isn't sales more about finding the right general access and gaining favorable access?"

Stan was right behind him and smugly interjected, "Mackenzie, let me guess. You picked up a new sales book with some new terms and it has some sales formula that you think will make a difference. Just because some book tells you to do something, doesn't mean it works in the real world." Stan smiled patronizingly at her and nodded to Mr. Garcia.

Mr. Garcia chimed in, "Stan's right. Books simplify sales into sales formulas so that they can sell books." Mr. Garcia and Stan exchanged glances.

Mackenzie felt her embarrassment rising, but kept as calm as she could, "I am trying to learn as much as I can from a few businessmen who have walked this road and remember what it was like to be in my shoes." She kind of spit out the sentence, frustrated that they weren't taking her seriously and mad at herself for asking a risky question.

"Interesting. You know, I lived in this city for most of my life. Who are these so-called businessmen you're learning from?" Stan asked, doubt dripping in his voice.

"JD Anderson and Bill Reichardt," Mackenzie stated.

Stan narrowed his eyes at her. Mr. Garcia lifted his eyebrows, revealing his surprise and asked, "JD and Bill? You know JD and Bill? How do you know JD and Bill?"

"I met JD at a cycling club, and he introduced me to Bill," Mackenzie answered.

"Wow. Stan, did you know about this? We've got a tiger in our midst. JD and Bill. I have so many stories about both of those guys; it would make your head spin. They are legendary. Hey, Stan, I'm going to take a few minutes with Mackenzie here. Let's plan on postponing lunch until 2pm. I'll text you when I'm ready to go."

Stan remained, dumbfounded. Mr. Garcia waved his hand, "It's just lunch, Stan. If you're hungry, you can take someone else. I've got to hear about this."

Stan cleared his throat. "No problem. I'll postpone lunch. I have a few deals to work on anyway." He quickly left the conference room.

Mr. Garcia turned back to Mackenzie. "Never mind Stan, he's

a bit territorial. I bet you he's been trying to get a meeting with JD or Bill for years." Mr. Garcia laughed, "I like your spirit, Mackenzie. You're a competitor; that's why I wanted Stan to hire you. Your numbers haven't been good, but I'm glad to see that you do still have that fire I read in your cover letter. I especially liked what you shared about your college competing days; I used to do a bit of running myself...

"But back to JD and Bill. Those two walk their talk. So, tell me about these terms they've taught you. I haven't heard those terms before. General and favorable something? What are those terms?" Mr. Garcia sat down and motioned for Mackenzie to sit with him and begin talking.

Mackenzie finally relaxed. *A question is rarely a question*, she reminded herself, then began, "Mr. Garcia, I want you to think back to being 14 year old Tony. Do you remember when you took your first scouting trip to the area of big yards and houses?"

"You are intent on taking me back there, huh? Okay, I'll go along. As 14 year old *Antonio*, I just had a feeling that if I wanted to build my business, I'd need to go where my friends weren't going. You see, my friends saw me making money mowing lawns, so they started their own businesses, and I lost a few customers. I decided that I had to go somewhere new where they wouldn't go."

"Exactly," Mackenzie echoed. "You knew where the big houses were, but those big shot owners didn't know you. So you had to position yourself to move from general access to favorable access within your suspect pool. What did you do first?"

"Interesting way of putting it," Mr. Garcia admitted. "Yes, I went up to the doors and knocked. And was told 'no' by every single house that day and the day after and the day after that. They all had professional lawn care services."

Mackenzie nodded and waited for him to continue.

"Then, I went back the next week, and I saw a 'for sale' sign on one of the lawns. I knew from observing homes being sold, that when people move in, their lawn care becomes very low on their priority list because there are so many other things to attend to. So I watched and waited. When the new family finally moved in, I just started mowing their lawn. I didn't ask. The grass was long, and it needed to be mowed. So I just mowed it." Mr. Garcia laughed. "I ran out of gas halfway through!"

"I walked up to the woman who looked like the owner and asked, 'Do you have a gas can I can borrow?' She was running around directing the movers and yelled at one of the movers to find the gas can.

"I ran as fast as I could to the gas station and back. I didn't finish that lawn until late that evening, and I walked home. I didn't ask for payment; I walked home that night with my mower. I went back the next week and did the same thing.

"This time, I wrote 'Garcia's Lawn Service' and my home phone number on a piece of paper and handed it to the woman. She asked, 'How much do I owe you?' And I said, 'Señora, I would like to take care of your yard every week. How much would you like to pay?' She told me a price. I nodded and said I'll be back next week. She ran after me with the money, and I said, 'We hadn't settled a price yet. You can start paying me next week.' She smiled the nicest smile at me. The next week, she told me that after I finished mowing that I should go next door and ask to take care of that yard. By the end of the summer, one new neighbor had convinced half of the street to use my lawn care business."

Mackenzie nodded with understanding, "I'm simplifying your story here, but it sounds to me like you positioned yourself, made deposits, moved from general access to favorable access, built trust that prompted referrals, and created demand-pull. Doing all of that as a 14 year old shows me that you were an early genius in sales!" She smiled.

Mr. Garcia chuckled, leaned back in his chair and rubbed his chin, then said, "If you had just told me your conclusion without tying it to my lawn care business, I probably would have argued with you. Hmmm. Positioning, deposits, general access, favorable access, demand-pull. Is this what JD and Bill have taught you?"

Mackenzie responded, "Mr. Garcia, there's a lot more to what JD and Bill have taught me. And you're right, without real life examples, the steps to demand-pull seem too simple and don't seem like they would work. If there were a way for us to work together to try out these steps at OnBoardMobile, then would you be willing to test them out?"

"Sounds like an interesting experiment. I think we could run a little test; sure," Mr. Garcia shrugged in agreement.

"Great. In order to do that, I need to ask a few additional questions." Mackenzie didn't know what her first question would be. She stalled by grabbing a pen and a scrap of paper from her purse, mind whirring. She didn't have the perfect question, but went with the first information-gathering question in her mind, "Can you help me with understanding which industries experience the greatest benefit from using our product?"

"Well, really any industry can benefit. But I've heard the most compelling feedback from businesses who have employees and small locations dispersed throughout cities or states, desperate to keep their independence yet still desire connection to the community within the company. Convenience store chains, fast food chains, independent distributors, multiple location manufacturers, businesses like that."

"Interesting. You mentioned distributors," Mackenzie pounced. "Just a shot in the dark here, but do you happen to know anyone from Whitman Distributors?"

"Whitman. I think so; it's been a while. Anyone in particular that you're thinking of?

"Ted Whitman, the CEO, or the HR Director, Karen Smith?"

"Ted Whitman," Mr. Garcia repeated. "Yes, vaguely know

him, not well. Karen Smith. Yes, I definitely know her. Her husband and I used to play golf together. Karen didn't love golf, but she was quite a runner and really into yoga a few years back. So tell me about Whitman."

Mackenzie briefed him on their distribution and her insight into their employee retention. Then she asked, "May I tell you a quick story about Karen?" Mr. Garcia nodded and Mackenzie detailed the meeting she had with Karen not giving her the time of day.

"Yep, Karen's a tough one. Not much into small talk. Hmm, Whitman Distributing. That would be a good fit with OnBoard-Mobile. Good thinking."

"Mr. Garcia, if there were a way for you to call Karen and ask her to give me one more chance, would you be willing to do that?"

"Sure. I don't have much time, so let's just call her right now. That work?"

"That would be great," Mackenzie finally exhaled, relieved that he continued to say yes.

Mackenzie looked up her number, dictated it, and took a deep breath.

Mr. Garcia's voice was upbeat, "Karen Smith! It's been a long time. This is Tony Garcia. My wife hasn't been running much lately, but she sends you her regards. Karen, please give me a call back at your convenience. I'm in town visiting the OnBoard-Mobile sales office here and talked with a Miss Mackenzie Jones. She says she made a fool of herself in front of you and would like another opportunity to meet with you. If I know you, I know you'll open the door again for a second chance. Looking forward to catching up. My number…"

Mackenzie's cheeks flushed while hearing him throwing her under the bus but she knew it was worth it. She swallowed hard.

"Thanks, Mr. Garcia," Mackenzie managed to say.

"No problem. What's next?" he asked.

Mackenzie presented her next question, "When she calls you back, could you tell her to show me her Work Comp ex-mod?"

"What? Why would you want to see that?" Mr. Garcia questioned.

Mackenzie explained the correlation JD taught her about.

"Well, that's a new angle. Sure, I can do that." Mr. Garcia looked at his watch. "Now, I have a favor to ask you."

Mackenzie nodded.

"I'd like you to send me JD and Bill's contact info, so I can drop them a line. Next time I'm in town, I'd like you to set up a meeting for us."

"Will do," she confirmed.

"Mackenzie, this has been most interesting. As you know, hiring this sales team was my idea, so I've been more involved than most CEOs with deciding who was hired and keeping updated on your progress. To be frank, Stan hasn't painted the best picture of you. But, I like what I'm hearing from you.

"It's been a long time since I've thought about what it's like to walk door to door, and I may have forgotten that it wasn't just my persistence that won me clients."

Mackenzie's thoughts tunneled toward her next goal, "Mr. Garcia, you've directed OnBoardMobile to capture training from both internal and external experts. Our clients' employees have recognized that there is power with using OnBoardMobile at just the right time, on their devices, with the click of a button. When we get our product into the right hands, our clients love it. But, a number of us on this new sales crew are having trouble just getting someone to answer a call and talk to us. In your opinion, do you think we have room for improvement in our own internal sales training techniques?"

"The last three months have told me that we definitely have room for improvement on our internal sales training," Mr. Garcia nodded.

"Mr. Garcia, if there were a way for me to capture these sales Steps & Rules from a trusted source and use that in our internal training, then would you be willing to explore that?"

Mr. Garcia's mouth turned down with his thinking. "That's an interesting thought. I'm very willing to explore that."

"Great. So, just one more question," she stated.

"Certainly," he agreed.

"If I drafted the script, then would you be open to me setting up a few trial video clips?" she asked.

He responded, "I'd love that. I'll talk to our marketing and training department, and we'll see what they can line up in terms of budget."

"Mr. Garcia, if you make the initial call to the training department for lining up a budget, I will follow up and make it happen."

"Well, then it's a plan. I'll call them from the airport today." Mr. Garcia paused then spoke again, "Mackenzie, I don't believe I've ever agreed to so much in such a short period of time. I'm not quite sure how we got here. But... I like it. I'm leaving now before I agree to anything else!" They both laughed.

"I'll tell Stan that I've got you on a special project. That should give you some breathing room. Keep me updated on your progress with Whitman Distributing."

"Will do. Thank you, Mr. Garcia."

ROAD RASH

Chapter 42

Mackenzie felt like she was finally in a race where she had a chance to win. Her mind was fueled with ideas of how she could make the next deposits towards Karen, Wayne, and Mr. Garcia. She felt momentum increasing. She felt the pull of the draft. She was invigorated.

She ran into Tommy, whose left cheek was still slightly swollen from his dental procedure, "Mackenzie! Ballsy in that meeting. You okay? I mean, they didn't fire you, did they?"

She thought about how that might have looked like a firing meeting. She laughed. "Thanks for asking, Tommy. It's all good. And by the way, how's your tooth?"

"Oh yeah, I've meant to tell you. Wow, that was the best recommendation. Dr. Evan showed me all the decay and explained everything to me. It was pretty bad. I'm glad you told me to get it done quickly; it was definitely not going to get better on its own. What a cool guy. And, I set up an appointment with him to talk about being a customer of OnBoard. I'm pretty stoked! They won't be a big client, but I think he'll be able to refer me to a few more clients, so I think it will be worth it. I can't thank you enough, Mackenzie!"

Mackenzie felt sucker-punched. If anyone should get a sales appointment with Dr. Evan, it should have been her. She was the one making referrals to Dr. Evan; she was making the deposits so she should be the one gaining favorable access, not Tommy. She steamed. She hadn't thought she had made enough deposits yet to ask for the referrals. *Didn't JD say I had to go slow to go fast? It looks like slow lost the race on this one,* she said to herself. She internally kicked herself and forced a smile.

"That's great, Tommy. Good work," she managed to say, despite feeling like the draft had just been replaced with a strong headwind. She told herself that she'd have to work harder and faster to catch the draft again.

The day became a blur of activity including follow-up calls with Karen, the OnBoard training team, and setting the agenda for her upcoming meeting with Wayne.

CROSS TRAINING
Chapter 43

She shot out of bed the next morning for the Dynamo meet-up. On her way to the ride, she decided that she would sign up for the cycling race. The race was that upcoming weekend. She was certainly not in peak performance, but this would be a test to determine how much more training she needed to rise to the next level.

She didn't see JD on the ride, despite looking everywhere for him. She really wanted to ask about what he would do in the scenario where a co-worker stole his lead. She thought to herself, *should I fight back for that lead? Or should I let it go and move on?*

She thought about her lead throughout the ride, riding harder than usual, releasing her pent-up frustration. Wes sprinted up to her on the last stretch and, in between heavy breaths commented, "You're riding hard today. You racing this weekend?"

"Yeah," she grunted. She didn't want to chit-chat but decided to continue the small talk. "I've never raced on a bike," she panted, "so I have no idea what to expect."

He nodded and kept breathing.

She felt prompted, "Hey, Wes, do you know JD?"

"Well, sure," he breathed out, "Doesn't everyone?"

"Guess so," she breathed, "You see him this morning?"

"Not here," he paused. "Overheard. Went. To hospital."

"JD's in the hospital?" she shouted.

"No. A friend," he panted back.

"Oh," she sighed, relieved.

"Yeah. Someone. Named Bill," he added.

"Bill? Bill Reichardt?" she choked.

"I dunno. Something about stairs," Wes huffed.

"Oh no," she started to panic. "I've gotta go!" she yelled at Wes as she pushed her pedals even harder and left him behind.

Her mind was reeling from the news. Falling down stairs when you're over 80 would not have a good outcome. *What if Bill is in a coma? What if he never recovers? No! We haven't even gotten started!* She needed him. Her whole plan centered on him. She pushed and pulled her pedals, deciding to head straight to the nearest hospital. If he was at a different hospital, she'd bike to the next one. The three main hospitals in Des Moines were all in a five mile radius of downtown.

She arrived at the hospital and didn't know where to park her bike. She didn't have a lock, but she didn't care. She left it on the bike rack and ran into the main entrance and thought: *If someone steals my bike today, so be it. I have more important things to worry about right now.*

Mackenzie spotted a woman at the main desk with a round face and a kind smile. "Good morning, I'm really hoping you can help me. I was just informed that my grandfather fell down the stairs and they didn't tell me which hospital he was admitted to. Can you please help me?" Mackenzie pleaded.

The receptionist warmly responded, "Sure, honey. What's his name?"

"Bill Reichardt," Mackenzie answered.

"Bill is your grand-daddy?" The woman cocked her head to the side.

"Yes," she lied, "Is he here?"

"He must have a lot of relatives," she shook her head and laughed. "They brought 'im in last night, and it wasn't an hour before all sorts a people started showing up, sayin' they cousins and grandkids o' Mr. Reichardt. I don't know who this guy is, but people like 'im so much they want to be related to 'im," she winked at Mackenzie. "We had to kick everyone out at 9 PM last night and regular visiting hours don't start until 8 AM," she paused.

Mackenzie looked at her phone which read 7:20 AM. She decided she'd wait. "Is he okay?"

"Yeah, he broke his leg last night. He's recovering on the 3rd floor, room 323," she winked again.

THE DRIVETRAIN
Chapter 44

Mackenzie took off her cycling shoes, glad to live in a town where kindness mattered. "Thank you!" she shouted as she slid in her socks to the elevators. As she punched the button for the elevator, a wave of relief washed over her. *Thank God it's not something serious*, she thought. She felt a pang of guilt realizing that she had been more initially worried about what he could do for her, rather than for his own well-being.

As she walked down the 3rd floor halls, she thought about how it didn't matter what happened with her work project. What really mattered was that Bill would get better.

She heard his unmistakable, bellowing laugh reverberate off the vinyl hospital floor. "Yep, Bill is here," she murmured. She raised her fist to knock at the half-opened door but hesitated as the laughter died down, and Bill's voice spoke with emotion cracking, "It's been a good run, hasn't it?"

"It sure has, Coach. It sure has. I heard that your kids are flying in today. It's not over, ya hear? Don't you go packing up your bags. We still have a lot of work to do. You can't quit now."

"I know. I've never quit on you, and I'm not about to start. But at some point, we have to let go, ya know?"

Mackenzie was frozen in place, barely breathing, as she listened to the exchange of words back and forth between these two men she barely knew, yet had so much impact on her life in such a short amount of time. She had grown up without strong male role models; getting to know these two men had restored some sense of hope that there were men out there who stuck around when times turned tough.

Mackenzie shifted her gaze back down the hallway to walk away. She didn't belong in that hospital room. She didn't deserve to be there. The two men shared a bond like father and son. She was just someone who was grasping for something to hold on to. JD broke the heavy silence.

"Nope. Not yet, Coach," JD cleared his throat. "Hey, do you remember the time when you went to the Willkie House to find Big T?"

"Oh, Big T, he was somethin,' wasn't he?"

Mackenzie turned back towards the door. The emotional tide had turned. She didn't know what to think about the earlier emotional exchange. *Bill just broke his leg, he's fine.* She encouraged herself to stay and express her hope for him to recover quickly.

She knocked on door 323. Bill hollered, "Come on in! Party's in here!"

She timidly walked into the room. The sunlight shined in from the window and reflected the glistening of their eyes.

"Mackenzie? Well, good morning to you!" Bill shouted from his hospital bed, surprised to see her. They both looked different. Bill looked older with hospital gown draped on his body, casted leg lifted up on a pulley and a deflated old football in his hands. JD looked tired. His eyes were puffy and red. He quickly looked down at his Styrofoam cup with steam billowing from the top.

"Hi Bill, JD. So sorry to interrupt. I was just at the cycling ride and heard that you fell down some stairs, Bill. I biked over right away. I'm so glad to hear you're okay."

JD and Bill exchanged glances. "Well, they say that a broken bone heals stronger. So I figure after this heals, I'll get to lose that damn cane!"

JD switched the subject. "Mackenzie, that's nice of you to drop by. How'd you find the room before visiting hours?"

"I said I was Bill's granddaughter." As she spoke those words, she realized that maybe she had pushed herself over the line by barging her way into the hospital room.

Bill smiled, "You do have a lot of potential as a salesperson. Good push for position, Mackenzie!"

Mackenzie was relieved with his gracious comment to alleviate the awkwardness she felt. She focused on the football in Bill's hands and blurted, "You guys playing some football in here or does that one have a story?"

"Everything has a story," JD laughed. "If that football could talk, you'd be here for days!"

Bill interjected, "Mackenzie, I told you the story about me going to the Firestone Tire plant for the first time, right?"

"Yeah, with the GM of Firestone, right?"

"Yep, that's the one. Do you remember what happened there?" Bill asked.

"Sure. You saw a group of young delinquents skipping school and smoking cigarettes. You told them that whoever could catch the football could keep it."

"Yep. Guess which delinquent caught that football?"

Mackenzie's mouth suddenly dropped, making the connection. She pointed slowly at JD and asked, "JD, you're Red?"

JD nodded. "I try not to hold onto memorabilia, but I've held onto that old football. That was the day someone saw something in me that I didn't see in myself," JD's voice trailed off, and he started to clear his throat again.

Mackenzie blinked furiously to keep the tears from rolling

down her cheeks. She finally understood why JD had carved out time for a nobody like her. Decades ago, he recognized that someone saw potential in him and had made a point to show him he could choose a different path for his life by learning from someone who was willing to teach.

Bill broke the silence, "Alright, alright. Let's not go down sentimental lane, here. I just thought it would be fun for her to know that when you show initiative, people take notice. And when the right people notice, they will help you to succeed. But enough of that, we need to switch the subject. Mackenzie, it's up to you. Tell us a joke, a story, something about work. Quickly. I'm not good with emotional stuff."

CAT 5 TATTOO

Chapter 45

Mackenzie faltered for words. She was terrible at telling jokes, and she couldn't think of any funny stories. So she started, "Well, I did talk with my CEO yesterday, and that went better than I thought it would."

"Great. Tell us about that," Bill coached.

Mackenzie began, "He was not exactly happy that I called him out on his pep talk about knocking on as many doors as possible, that it was all about the numbers."

"Bold move!" Bill chuckled.

"Yeah, he and my sales manager were about to lecture me about how what I read in books doesn't mean that it translates in the real world when I told him I wasn't getting my info from a book; I was learning from two distinguished businessmen," she smiled, looking at Bill and JD. "They laughed and asked who these two 'businessmen' were." She motioned with air quotes and continued, "I told them, JD Anderson and Bill Reichardt.

"Their smirks dropped from their faces like someone slapped them. My CEO then postponed his lunch appointment with my sales manager and sat with me for the next 20 minutes to hear about what you've been teaching me. My CEO, Tony Garcia, said, 'those two guys walk their talk.'"

"Wait. Tony Garcia is your CEO? No way! Well, isn't that a hoot!" exclaimed JD.

"You know him?" Mackenzie asked.

"Sure do. It's been a long time, but we were on the Boys and Girls Club board for a number of years together. Good guy. Really hard worker. So, I've got to know: did you ask him to open the door to any of his contacts?"

"I did." She paused, and then added, "He threw me under the bus…but as you said, humility is a good thing."

"Well, I guess that's one way of doing it. Ya know, I do remember that as he moved up the chain of command in his last company, he started to get what I call the C-suite curse."

"The C-suite curse? What's that?" Mackenzie asked.

JD answered, "When you move up to the C-suite, it's quite a boost to the ego. Add to that, about 90% of everything you say or do as an exec, people start turning into yes-robots, at least to your face. You get used to that positive reinforcement and getting your way. Rejection becomes less and less tolerable. Even if he or she started off in sales, you'd have a hard time getting any C-suite exec back to sales where rejection is an everyday occurrence."

Mackenzie could see how that might happen. Most people want to get as far away from rejection as possible. She also remembered Mr. Garcia's selective memory. He'd wanted to claim credit himself and initially refused to remember how his path to success had involved establishing and maximizing both general and favorable access.

JD had more to add, "We see this a lot in non-profit boards. Take, for example, raising money. As a board member, we are often asked to fundraise. It's hard to call on your friends because then they may start thinking you're into the relationship for what you're going to get. This is why fundraisers are usually held with dinner and drinks. That way, we invite our friends to dinner, and someone else asks for the money. It doesn't hurt that alcohol is involved strategically and that your friends' egos are applauded when they stand up publicly in an auction and spend a bunch of money on an item."

Bill laughed. Mackenzie's eyebrows lifted in surprise. She had never heard this perspective.

JD continued, "On the flip side, it's hard when friends say, 'No, I'm not going to do business with you.' It's a personal stab to the heart and ego. This is why the C-suite wants to be removed from the direct sale. It is hard being rejected. This is why it's important for most CXOs to be one person removed.

"This is also why it is so important that marketing and sales overlap their efforts. The job of marketing is to first create favorable access and then to build demand-pull. Marketing can do this in many ways: by promotion of the CEO, promotion of the sales team, or promotion of the product. Most CEOs and owners are good at promoting themselves, but they have trouble giving up control and transferring their favorable access to others. Take Bill for example."

Bill quickly cocked his head towards JD and remarked, "You're really going to punch the old man when he's stuck in a gurney?"

TEAM TIME TRIAL
Chapter 46

JD nodded to Bill, "Yep," then turned to face Mackenzie. "Bill was the perfect example of control curtailing the power of favorable access. He was masterful at promoting himself, his sales team, and his product on those TV ads. Do you think he ever walked out of his safe store and into a corporate setting to promote his product to his direct customers? Did he ever let his sales team promote his product directly to those in his favorable access?"

Mackenzie looked at Bill. Bill laughed. "Hell, no. I had a bad case of the C-suite curse!"

JD nodded. "Bill was too comfortable with the TV ads because that removed him enough from the direct sale, and he had control over those TV ads."

Bill replied, "True. But if it ain't broke, don't fix it!"

"You're right, it wasn't broken…at first," JD said to Bill then turned back to Mackenzie. "Bill experienced a huge increase in sales after the TV ads. But then what?" JD glanced at Bill again with his question and continued talking to Mackenzie, "Then things cooled down, and over time it wasn't as effective. So, Bill decided to promote himself in other ways and to continue to push his name in front of people. He ran for political office and found his way into newspapers and news coverage using his favorable access where he voiced his opinion on controversial topics. But, it would have been a lot simpler and more powerful if he had leveraged his favorable access in a way that allowed his salespeople to go out and get in front of his prospects in a business setting. He could have exponentially increased the store's favorable access."

Bill shook his head and said, "Maybe. But I liked doing it my way."

"Sure," JD replied, "Because you needed that control and wanted all eyes on you."

Bill guffawed, "You're lucky I'm in a cast, Red. I might be old, but I could still take you."

JD grinned at Bill then turned back to Mackenzie, "We have to choose our battles wisely. Timing is everything." JD laughed and went to get Bill a glass of water.

Bill took the water and sarcastically growled, "A Coors Light would be better."

Mackenzie marveled at the candid honesty that these two men shared with each other. Their banter made her think that they had argued about this topic before with JD apparently losing that battle. She decided to probe, "I'm sensing that you two have had heated discussions about this before. Did your arguments ever threaten to sever your friendship?"

"Ha! Red didn't talk to me for about five years after college. You want to tell her about that?" Bill chuckled.

"Which part, Bill? I could tell a few different sides of those stories," JD looked sideways at Bill.

"I've done some things in the past that I'm not proud of but might as well bring 'em all out in the open so someone else can learn from them," Bill shrugged in his hospital gown.

"Some things don't need to be repeated," JD replied to Bill then turned to Mackenzie. "Trust takes a lifetime to build and a moment to break. I'll give you the condensed version, Mackenzie."

JD motioned for Mackenzie to sit down as he sat down in the other chair and propped his feet up on Bill's hospital bed, "I was taking marketing and accounting courses in college. My plan was to use what I learned and help Bill take his business to the next level. I would test what I was learning while working in the store during the summer. Bill wanted nothing of the sort. He was doing just fine without me changing his business model. I figured that I had learned all I could from Bill. He was too old and set in his ways. He was going to miss out by not using new marketing techniques. I was young and arrogant. So we had an argument at the store that might still be ringing in people's ears. It wasn't pretty." JD and Bill exchanged looks and laughed.

JD brought his feet down to the vinyl floor, "I stormed out of the store and vowed never to return. I was stubborn and decided I wasn't going to use any relationship which tied to Bill in any way. But, everywhere I turned, each relationship had some kind of connection with Bill. So I kept looking. I was just seeking a summer job at that point, but I couldn't get one.

"I went back to Iowa City and washed dishes in a restaurant. While scrubbing pans, I thought about the old saying, 'It's not what you know, it's who you know.' And that's when I started remembering Bill's stories, writing them down, and thinking about what he did to get to where he was. And I realized that Bill had positioned himself, in so many situations, to build trust first. That was the start for me thinking that it's *not* just who you know; it's all about who knows you and trusts you.

"But, I was still too proud to apologize to Bill at that time. If he wanted to do it his way, he would do it his way. If I wanted to do things differently, I needed to chart my own course. If I wanted to convince someone to do something different, I'd have to show by example and invite him to join me.

"The next summer, I landed an internship with an insurance

brokerage in Des Moines. I worked my tail off trying to show Bill that he was wrong, that I knew more, and that I'd be more successful using my way. A few years in, I found out that I got the internship because Bill put in a good word for me. It was then that I swallowed my pride and walked back into Bill's store to thank him. I realized I still had a lot to learn from him. Book knowledge alone didn't make me smarter. Experience, failure, and applying what we learn from failure make the keys that open the doors to wisdom. And Bill was full of that kind of wisdom!"

Bill shook his head and laughed.

PACELINE
Chapter 47

JD shared, "I thought I could take what I learned from college and make vast improvements to the way business was being done. Experience in the real world reminded me that college doesn't offer a sales degree. Colleges offer marketing, branding, and advertising courses. They teach that the 'right' marketing, branding and advertising leads to sales. We learn about spreadsheets and balance sheets with the top line being income, but we don't necessarily learn about how to bring in the sales that make the income. We learn that if you do a good job marketing, branding, advertising, you'll get sales. Once you're a salesperson, you realize that's not the case at all. As you've learned, sales are really about creating favorable access and creating demand-pull."

Mackenzie nodded in agreement. He said exactly what she felt about her college learning experience. If only she could have learned JD's lessons in her marketing courses.

"The 'right' marketing can lead to sales if you use marketing to create favorable access for your salespeople. If marketing doesn't bridge the gap between their advertising and sales, the salesperson has to jump the gap or build the bridge, which takes a lot of practice or a lot of time and expertise.

"Marketing can create favorable access in many ways. Marketing can promote the CEO, promote the company, or the product, as Bill did. Or if you're particularly savvy, marketing can promote the current customers; this can become a deposit for your customers while simultaneously connecting them even closer to your company and product, further cementing their loyalty. But that's a topic for a different day.

"Whichever route is promoted, the main goal of marketing is to create favorable access for the salesperson to get a meeting with the prospect, which you'll remember is Step 3: Favorable access to get a meeting. The favorable access of the CEO, company or product should be transferred to the salesperson to make this process most effective. The salesperson needs to know that this transfer is a transfer of trust. This trust is extremely valuable and needs to be handled with the utmost respect.

"There are expectations to set with the salespeople. If the expectations are clear, then the CEOs or those in a favorable position can take their influence and transfer their access to the person below or behind them. It's just like riding in the cycling paceline. If employees are on the same paceline team, the sales process should be a circular relationship; pull, then let the next rider pull through so the front-runner can recover for the next pull. Just like marketing to sales, sales to marketing; it keeps rotating through. One department creates demand-pull for the other department. There is no draft riding solo."

Yes! Mackenzie found her earlier frustration with Stan and Mr. Garcia's approach justified. She summarized her thoughts in her mind, *it takes a sales team, a paceline, to build and capitalize on general and favorable access. The most successful salespeople simply cannot achieve solo what is only possible with the synergy of a team, all riding forward, together, towards the same goal. That was the disconnect I've been feeling.*

There was a knock at the door, and a loud voice hollered. "It's time to shut up and eat!"

Mackenzie quickly recognized Randy Duncan, Bill's friend, former campaign manager, and former Hawkeye quarterback, as he walked in with a nurse. Bill shouted to his friend, "It's about time! Red won't stop talking, and I'm hungry!"

The nurse looked puzzled to see the young woman in the room. Both Randy and the nurse had on surgical masks and handed them to JD and Mackenzie. "I thought I told you to wear masks. Do I need to start limiting privileges?" she said sternly.

"Bill wouldn't let me wear it. It was freaking him out," JD responded sheepishly.

"Well, better to be freaked out than get an infection. Put them on now. You especially, young lady."

Mackenzie was confused. *Surgical masks? For a broken leg? Is this some sort of new hospital regulation?*

"Mr. Reichardt, I need to talk to you about your options and where we need to move you. Who do you want in the room for this discussion?"

It was clear that it was Mackenzie's time to go, so she quickly made her exit. "Bill, JD, wonderful to see you. Mr. Duncan, a pleasure to see you as well."

They all nodded.

As Mackenzie started to walk out of the room, Bill shouted after her, "Hey, Mackenzie, call Wayne and tell him I want you to meet with him!"

Mackenzie turned back to him, nodded, and gave him a thumbs up. A lump had worked its way to her throat, and she knew she shouldn't try to say anything. Bill obviously had something more than a broken leg, and yet, there he was, remembering her needs. JD's comments about it being 'a good run' started to give her an eerie feeling. Tears started to well up in her eyes. This time, the tears were not for missing out on what Bill could do for her. She was crying because she feared that would be the last time she would get to see him.

As she rode home to change for work, she thought about how short her time with Bill was, yet how much she had learned from him. He cared about others and he showed his care through how he lived. She was now more determined than ever to capture and preserve Bill and JD's lessons and legacy.

THE SPRINT
Chapter 48

Mackenzie's sense of urgency had kicked into high gear. Time was short. She was ready to make things happen, and she was ready to employ every Step & Rule JD taught her.

As soon as she arrived at the office, she called Wayne. He wasn't available, but she did not leave a message. She was determined to call throughout the day until he picked up. In between those calls, she called the OnBoardMobile's training department, a dozen leads where she felt she could create favorable access, and Karen Smith, the HR Director at Whitman Distributing. She called on rotation until she was talking personally with the person she intended to call.

In her calls to OnBoard's marketing and training, she used their CEO's name and thoughts as if he was in the room. She was clear with her questions and listened intently. Although she fumbled quite a few "If there were a way…." alignment questions, she kept practicing. She was making progress.

Finally, Wayne took her call. "Wayne, I don't think that Bill Reichardt has had an opportunity to call you yet. My name is

THE SPRINT

Mackenzie Jones, and I visited Bill in the hospital this morning. He told me to set up a meeting with you. Is today or tomorrow a good time to meet with you?"

"What? Bill is in the hospital? Is he okay?" Wayne exclaimed his questions.

Mackenzie knew to keep it upbeat, "He's in good spirits with his broken leg."

"That's a relief. Alright, I'm sorry, what's your name again, and what are we meeting about?" Wayne asked.

"My name is Mackenzie Jones, and Bill thought I could be helpful to you in regards to the retention of your employees. This younger generation is hard to retain; am I right?"

"Don't even get me started on young people these days. We are having a tough time recruiting and retaining our younger workers. My best store manager was just talking to me about that this morning. Sure, let's meet. I'll bring in Mike to tell you what he told me. How about this afternoon? Three o'clock?"

After Mackenzie hung up the phone, she stared at it. She was stunned; that kind of 'yes' had never happened before. It seemed too easy, too lucky. *Cheers to favorable access!* She looked at the time. She would finish a few more phone calls and then prepare for the meeting with Wayne.

For the fourteenth time that morning, she called Whitman Distributing, Karen's line. To her amazement, Karen answered the phone. Mackenzie began, "Hello Karen. This is Mackenzie Jones. As Tony Garcia said in his voicemail to you, I failed in my meeting with you, and I apologize. I would like to ask for your forgiveness and a second chance."

Mackenzie stopped to take a breath. Her heart was beating wildly. She was about to fill the silence when Karen spoke again. "Well, hello, Mackenzie. I appreciate and accept your apology."

An elongated pause followed. Mackenzie didn't know where to go next and babbled, "Tony said that you practice yoga. May I treat you to a yoga class of your choice and a coffee after the class?"

"Hmmm, I haven't been to yoga in a few months…" Mackenzie tensed as she felt the impending rejection, "…And I'd actually like to take you up on your offer. Yes, how's a 6 AM Monday morning class next week sound to you?"

"Perfect, I'll set it up and email you the details." Mackenzie breathed a sigh of relief after ending the call. This was a step in the right direction. Building trust with Karen looked to be a longer road, but at least she found a way to make her day better, and she was looking forward to a yoga class herself. Mackenzie imagined that she would really need someone to lead her through some deep stretching after her first cycling race in a few days.

She arched her back and took a deep breath. It was then that she noticed a package on her desk. In the three months she had worked in the office, she had never received a package. In the rush of the morning, she hadn't taken time to look at anything except her phone and computer screen. She picked it up and saw Luke's company logo on the return address.

Curious, she ripped into the package, wondering why Luke's company would send her anything. A familiar blue, orange, black, and white cycling jersey emerged. The block letters of "Dynamo Coffee," made her gasp. She hadn't told anyone about how much she wanted to have the Dynamo jersey.

A plain 3x5 note card fell out of the package. She read it silently, "Thought you might want one of these. – Luke."

She sat back in her chair, looking at the jersey. A wave of gratitude swept over her. She texted Luke, "Wow. Just received the most thoughtful gift from a friend. Thank you."

He texted back, immediately, "Glad you like it. You look like you're committed to the team and I thought you might like a jersey."

THE SPRINT 237

She texted back, "A brand new jersey! Just in time for my first bike race! Think it'll make me faster?"

He texted, "Ha! It may not, but you will look faster."

Mackenzie thought back to the night he invited her to the cycling group after she confessed her work woes to him over a few beers. At the time, joining a cycling group didn't seem like anything to help her turn things around at work. But now, she saw it differently. Luke's invitation to something new had reignited her health both physically and mentally. Being ditched the first day, making a fool of herself with the fall, and failing to keep up but not quit, had turned into opportunities to allow people to come alongside her and give her a push in the right direction. Learning from failure and persevering to keep moving had allowed her to embrace small changes; those small changes really had made a big difference.

She held up the jersey again and smiled, thinking about Luke. She and Luke had an odd friendship. Dating was out of the question because Mackenzie's friend had been Luke's girlfriend for a few years in college. Through the filter of her friend, she heard how self-centered he was. He was aloof and appeared underwhelmed with most people. He and Mackenzie had usually enjoyed their conversations, mostly because she would ask him questions about his projects. He was an interesting person to listen to because he was a deep thinker; he had developed serious opinions and theories on subjects that mattered to him. He was a high achiever and loved to discuss ideas on how to improve efficiencies of systems, especially in his field of technology. But, he was often robotic in his approach to life, forgetting that people had feelings. His emotionless nature was the biggest turn-off for Mackenzie and had allowed them to easily remain platonic friends.

The unexpected gift took her by surprise. Not that a gift meant that she was now interested in him, but it did show her that he could think about others. He had a heart inside him somewhere. She liked her friends to have some emotion, and she did want to make sure he knew how much she appreciated the gesture.

She texted Luke again, "Want to meet up for a beer again anytime soon?"

His response was quick and concise, "Sounds good. Exile Brewing 7 PM next week. How's Tuesday?"

FOCUS

Chapter 49

As the next hours flew by, Mackenzie prepared for her meeting with Wayne. She researched and took notes on his clothing store locations, his company's history, and any articles she could find about Wayne.

She knew she needed an agenda for the meeting and to write it with Wayne and his sales manager's needs in mind. *I can't get what I want until they get what they want. So what is it that they want?*

She reviewed her notes on JD's Steps & Rules.

8 Steps of the Sales Process

1. Understand your general access.
2. Develop a plan to gain favorable access.
3. Leverage favorable access to get a meeting.
4. Set the agenda and then put the customer in control.
5. Build trust through dialogue.
6. Create alignment. Identify the problem and align what they need with what you can do for them.
7. Control the question and the direction.
8. Summarize and guide with next steps.

* Start with Step 1 in every new relationship.

8 Rules of the Paceline

1. You can't get what you want until they get what they want.
2. Go slow to go fast.
3. Questions are rarely questions. Understand the why.
4. Make significant deposits before withdrawing or asking for a loan.
5. Practice until the process becomes instinctive.
6. Communicate the value of your vision in their terms.
7. Provide perspective, not just content.
8. People don't care how much you know until they know how much you care.

*Terms to know – favorable access and demand-pull:

Favorable access opens the door between you and your prospect. Demand-pull increases the desire of your prospect to move through the door towards the sale.

With the Steps and Rules top of mind, she drafted her initial thoughts for the agenda.

- History: Hiring practice and retention
- Dark side: Difficulties in turnover
- Discovery: Retail industry trends
- Simple Solution: Depending on answers to above, align strategies, solutions, and game plan.

Mackenzie emailed Wayne the finalized agenda and a relevant HR article she had found on the costs of losing employees in the retail industry.

PART FIVE
Full Circle

LANDING A CLIENT
Chapter 50

She decided to go early to Wayne's store and buy an accessory. This way, she could make a quick deposit and observe how she was treated as a customer. A well-dressed twenty-something sales associate approached her. "May I help you find something today?"

"Oh, I'm just looking," Mackenzie returned.

"Okay. Let me know if you need any help finding something," the sales associate replied and then turned his back to re-straighten the jackets on hangers.

Mackenzie observed how this vague question did nothing to engage her with the store or the staff. This was a very different feeling than what she experienced at Reichardt's Clothing. She continued to browse and was ringing up a pair of socks when she recognized Wayne from the photo she researched on the internet.

She introduced herself exactly how Bill had taught her, making sure her handshake was firm, but not more firm than his, her eye contact was solid, and her smile was bright. Wayne, Mike, and Mackenzie walked to the back room and pulled up a few chairs next to a foosball table.

Mackenzie began, "Wayne, Mike, I am so grateful for your time. Mike, as I told Wayne, Bill sends his regards. So that I can be respectful of your time, I drafted up this agenda."

Mackenzie gave them both a copy of the short agenda, read it to them and said, "Is there anything you'd like to talk about specifically or add to this agenda?"

Wayne and Mike shrugged their shoulders and Wayne replied, "Thanks for emailing it earlier. Let's start at the top."

Mackenzie could see that Wayne was engaged but Mike looked disengaged. She decided to focus more of her energy on Mike. "Sounds good. Starting from the top, Mike, could you give me a quick summary of the roles you are responsible for?"

Wayne jumped in, "He's the Benefits Manager and Sales Leader. He's responsible for hiring, training, and retaining all of our employees across all of our stores."

Mackenzie wrote a few notes and responded, "Thanks, Wayne. Mike, in your position, tell me a little about the scope of your responsibilities."

Mike asserted himself before Wayne could speak for him, "We have twenty stores. Right now, I'm doing whatever it takes to keep our employees retained and working well. Basically, I spend most of my time extinguishing fires."

"Give me a few examples of what are you experiencing with your employees," Mackenzie requested.

"If it weren't for employees, my job would be easy," Mike sarcastically suggested.

Mackenzie and Wayne laughed as Mike continued, "I've tried everything to keep our employees. I've created a fun atmosphere, put a foosball table here in the backroom, and started Beer Fridays to create a social environment. When they leave, they tell me it's because they want to be paid more. But the crazy thing is some of them leave without even having their next job lined up! So they're going from our pay to absolutely nothing. It doesn't make sense. We shouldn't have this kind of turnover."

"What kind of turnover do you have?" Mackenzie asked.

Wayne interjected, "About 30%."

Mike gave him a sideways glance, "30%? 30% will leave. Then I have to personally fire about 20%! On average it's 50%. On a bad year, it's up to 75%."

"That's tough," Mackenzie empathized. "Have you ever calculated the cost of losing an employee?"

"The article you sent us is one of the main reasons I wanted to be at this meeting," Mike stated.

"I'm glad that was insightful. I brought another article for you about the savings of retaining good employees. Tell me, what does it take for you to replace a few employees?" Mackenzie gently inquired.

Mike took a deep breath, "We have to recruit, interview, vet, onboard them, put them through enrollment, and walk them through the handbook and training."

Mackenzie steered back to the numbers, "How many employees do you have in each store?"

"About ten or eleven. We hire a few additional each season," Mike replied.

"Okay," said Mackenzie, beginning the math problem in her head. "Let's say there are ten in each, times twenty stores. That's two hundred employees. So, on average, you lose one hundred per year to turnover. Is that correct?"

Both Wayne and Mike nodded slowly.

Mackenzie continued, "Per our industry data, the time to recruit, interview, hire, onboard and train a retail employee who is paid an estimated $35,000 salary, will cost, on the low side, about $5,000. Let's use two hundred employees and say your turnover is 50% average, so that's 100 employees per year. That's…$500,000." Mackenzie paused purposefully to let that number sink in.

"Yikes," Mike groaned.

Mackenzie knew to keep going, "And, as an estimate, what's an average price for a suit that you sell here?"

"Average? I'd say $1,000." Mike looked to Wayne to confirm. Wayne nodded.

"And what's your estimated margin on that suit?" Mackenzie asked.

"About 50%," Wayne chimed in, moving to the edge of his seat.

"So how many suits would you have to sell to cover the cost of losing your employees?" She paused and scratched out the math. "You'd have to sell one thousand suits."

"One thousand suits? That's more than we sell in a store over a year," Wayne stated incredulously.

"It'd be a lot more if we used dress shirts to cover it," Mike suggested.

"I've never thought of it this way," Wayne and Mike looked at each other.

"So, if there were a way to reduce your turnover by 50%, which is equivalent to selling 500 suits, then you would be interested?" Mackenzie offered.

"Are you kidding? You'd be the top sales associate in our company!" Wayne exclaimed.

Mike stated, "I'm intrigued. I don't have the time or budget to bring on an outside consultant. What does it cost to hire you?"

"A lot less than $500,000 a year." She smiled, and Wayne guffawed, slapping his knee. Mike still looked skeptical. Mackenzie continued, "But you asked that for a reason. Tell me why."

Mike blurted, "I have HIPPAA, Cobra, ADA, FMLA, sexual harassment, employee handbooks, job descriptions, gender equity, hiring, firing, benefits education, and benefits enrollment. You want me to spend more time training employees? I don't have time!"

"I agree, but if there were a way that it wouldn't take you any more time, then would that be of interest to you?" Mackenzie asked.

Mike almost yelled, "How does that work?"

Mackenzie replied calmly, "Our technology does the heavy lifting."

Wayne turned to Mike and said, "We need to hire her."

"With me, you get my company," Mackenzie added.

Mike pushed, "What does it cost to get?"

Wayne blurted, "Does it matter?!"

Mike retorted, "Of course it matters. It always matters."

Mackenzie didn't think the first meeting was where she should have them sign on the bottom line, nor had she followed the Steps exactly. But, it was clear that Wayne was ready. "Well, I have paperwork to do and would need to work with Mike before we formalize anything. Is there anything else stopping us from moving to the next steps?"

"No," Wayne deadpanned.

Mackenzie didn't hesitate. "I did bring a formal contract in case this happened. It has a $25,000 retainer and implementation fee. Then it is $5 per month, per employee."

"Five dollars a month per employee? We spend that much on free coffee for them." Wayne flipped the paper around and signed it.

THE NEXT LEVEL

Chapter 51

Mackenzie sped through the next day, fueled by her adrenaline to deliver the best customer service to her first client. The details were really coming together. Mr. Garcia congratulated Mackenzie on her win. He told her that he was pushing their marketing team to allocate resources to bring in Bill and JD's content to level up their sales process training.

When Thursday morning arrived, she was eager to get to the ride in order to tell Lisa that she had signed up to race with Dynamo. Mackenzie had recognized that her momentum started by getting outside her comfort zone and pushing herself in cycling.

Lisa was ecstatic about her news, "Alright, Z! This will be great! We really need your sprinting ability. Now, as you know, small changes make a big difference. You've been lugging around on that steel-framed Schwinn for weeks. I know you're fond of your bike, but that's like carrying dumbbells on your shoulders and riding uphill. That heavy frame is okay for training. Not for racing."

Mackenzie's heart sank. She couldn't afford a new bike. She

reasoned that she had been able to keep up and pull the group just fine with her Schwinn. She opened her mouth to argue with Lisa in order to avoid the conversation about her budget.

Lisa continued, "You're my size. If you're racing with me, you've got to be on your A-game, and that starts with having the right gear. We will need your power to pull for us. I've got my back-up bike on my car rack. Let's switch your bike with mine right now because you'll need to get used to it fast."

Mackenzie's heart lifted. Lisa already had a solution. As they neared Lisa's car, Mackenzie's jaw dropped in admiration of her back-up bike. The bike was similar to Lisa's first-slot racing bike, a custom-made Specialized racing bike. She was nervous about riding it because she knew the price tag was definitely more than her credit card limit. Before she even climbed onto the beautiful bike, she knew that the carbon frame and carbon-alloy wheels would be like trading a John Deere Gator for a Formula One racecar.

As she clicked in, her excitement grew. She couldn't wait for Saturday.

GETTING POSITIONED
Chapter 52

The race morning finally arrived. Mackenzie rode to the venue an hour early. She hadn't brought her phone because she didn't want any extra weight on her. She felt a little lost and naked without it. She fought the urge to find someone's phone to call Lisa and ask where they should meet. She opted instead to do her own warm-ups and get mentally prepared on her own.

This would be a road race with one loop of 26 miles on the county roads. She picked up her racing bib and packet. She studied the map. She paced. She stretched. She observed the other riders. Most were walking around in groups with matching jerseys, but no sign of Dynamo surfaced.

Then out of the corner of her eye, she spotted a woman with a long dark braid, wearing a blue Dynamo jacket who was bent over, adjusting her shoe. A purple helmet rested beside her.

Mackenzie walked a circle around the woman to get in her sight line. She mentally prepared her greeting as the woman began standing up. She waited for the woman to tilt her head up to see if she recognized her. As Mackenzie opened her mouth to say hello, the sunlight hit the top of her hair and reflected an almost-purple hue. Her heart sank. "Jules, right?"

Mackenzie extended her hand and forced the most genuine smile she could muster to Wes's girlfriend, whom she didn't like the first time and discovered she still felt the same way about her.

Jules did not seem to recognize Mackenzie, "Hi," she said as she shook Mackenzie's hand.

Mackenzie offered, "I'm Mackenzie, I met you at one of the Dynamo practice rides a few weeks ago. Are you riding with the Dynamo team today?"

"Oh. No, I'm not riding with Dynamo. I've put in a lot of hours training, and I want to be on a team that will bring me points so that I can move up to a higher category as quickly as possible. So I joined the team that will take me there," she replied, with a hint of contempt. Then, looking down at her Dynamo jacket, she peeled it off, unveiling a bright yellow jersey with a lightning bolt on the front, the logo of a local electrical contracting company. Team Electric.

Mackenzie could tell from her tone that she wasn't interested in continuing the conversation. "Oh, I thought Dynamo was one of the better teams in the area. Well, what do I know? I just bought my first cycling license for my first race!" She laughed, trying to break Jules' cold stare and offered, "Best of luck to you."

As Mackenzie walked off, her competitive instincts took over. *Well, I'll just have to show her she made the wrong choice. She has no idea what the Dynamo paceline is capable of doing together. You're going to eat our dust, Jules.*

Mackenzie looked back over her shoulder and saw Wes walking toward Jules. Mackenzie raised her hand in a wave to Wes then walked off in a different direction. Mackenzie didn't understand how a gentleman like Wes could be attracted to such a cold woman like Jules.

Before she psyched herself out of her competitive mindset, she decided to re-focus on the race before her. She was a trained competitor in running; she could translate her track racing preparations to cycling. She started to visualize her race. She reviewed everything she had learned in the past few weeks.

When you position yourself favorably in a group to use the draft, you allow yourself to use the power generated by the paceline around you. It was time to find the Dynamo team.

She circled the race site, scanning for the Dynamo logo. Finally, she spotted the team and quickly rode over. Lisa's brow was furrowed as she discussed something with Brenda. She overheard Lisa say, "Well, that's unfortunate, but we've got enough depth to cover…"

Lisa saw Mackenzie approach and yelled, "About time, Z! I hope you were getting your game face on. We've got our work cut out for us this morning if we want to be in this race."

Eager to please, Mackenzie responded, "I'm ready. What's up?"

"One of our lead riders came down with the flu last night. We're scrambling to figure out a revised strategy."

Mackenzie nodded, "If there were a way for me to help fill her role, then would you be interested in that?" She felt a little odd using the alignment question, but JD did tell her to practice.

"Ya know what? I think you can do it. Hey, Dynamo! Z is ready to roll this morning!"

The women turned towards Mackenzie. They gave her high fives and slapped her back. In the midst of this energy and enthusiasm, Mackenzie knew she'd ride hard for the team and not worry about her individual placement, or beating Jules. Helping her team meant more to her than her individual points.

"Well, aren't you a sight for sore eyes!" one rider exclaimed. Another commented, "I thought you were just with Dynamo to talk to JD. I didn't know you wanted to race!"

GETTING POSITIONED

Mackenzie didn't quite know how to handle that last comment. JD's words echoed in her mind: *keep above the fray*. She controlled the next questions, "How can I help? Where do you need me? Tell me the tactics for this race."

It was decided that she would be one of the four women to rotate pulling the paceline at the beginning of the race. She was to recover in the middle of the race, if she was still in the pack. Keep formation, keep the rotation. A few riders mentioned how much they wanted to beat Team Electric.

Jules' name was spit out of a few teammates' mouths. "She had the nerve to demand that we all work to get her in position to sprint the end. This is her first race! I heard she bought her way into Team Electric. What a wheel-sucker." Jules had clearly not left Dynamo on good terms.

Brenda pulled her aside and shared, "By the way, we don't expect you to be in the lead group past the mid-point. But, if you do make it, it's an all-out fight to the finish. Especially if you see a woman in a yellow jersey, leave it all out there."

She was speaking Mackenzie's language. Her track coaches over the years had told her that line dozens of times. Leave it all out on the track. That, she knew she could do.

Mackenzie was thrilled to race on Lisa's custom-made Specialized racecar. Mackenzie couldn't help but admire its beauty. She thought about JD's cost formula: Cost = Price - Value. If Mackenzie raced as fast as she had practiced on the Specialized bike, then the value was priceless, which made her re-think cost. *Totally worth it,* she grinned.

As they rolled their bikes to the start line, a guy started running towards the group. "Mackenzie! Hey! Mackenzie!"

Mackenzie turned towards the sound of her name and saw him. His hair was messy, his eyes shined brightly. He was out of breath as he reached her. "Hey. Heard you were racing today."

"Luke! What are you doing here?" Mackenzie blurted.

"Thought you might want someone to cheer you to victory," Luke offered with a genuine smile.

Mackenzie laughed, knowing there was no chance of her winning her first race. His cheeks blushed slightly. Most people wouldn't have noticed. But she had never seen Luke blush.

Mackenzie was surprised by this version of Luke standing before her. He seemed to be maturing into a new person over this past month. Then, he sent the unexpected gift. Now, both his unexpected presence and his unexpected emotions. She didn't know what to make of it, "Uh, really cool of you to be here. Thanks, Luke."

"I'll see you at the finish!" Luke yelled with uncharacteristic enthusiasm as he trotted off.

Mackenzie shook her head. *Yep, something is definitely up with him.* She shook her head, ready for the race. *I'll think about him later. Right now, it's race time.*

A DIFFERENT LINE
Chapter 53

Team Dynamo jockeyed as close as they could to the starting line with all of the other colorful jerseys. Mackenzie was so focused on staying near Lisa that she barely heard the starting announcement.

The race pace was fast right out of the gate. Mackenzie was surprised at her ability to not only keep up but to continue rotating up front. She still couldn't believe the difference the racing bike made in her speed. She felt like the racing bike was a powerful extension of her own body. *Who knew the right bike could make this much difference? Fit and quality really does matter.*

Suddenly the paceline shifted, and she adjusted too sharply, causing someone to shout, "Focus!" Mackenzie nodded and thought, *get your head back in the game, Mackenzie! Now is not the time to figure out JD's puzzles.* She quickly moved back into the paceline and focused on the road in front of her.

Mid-race, a breakaway group with three from Team Electric pulled away from the rest of the pack. Mackenzie's instincts were to get out of formation and try to catch them. Lisa yelled, "Z, easy!"

Mackenzie heeded her call, frustrated that their competitors were getting away. A few miles later, Lisa called the top four to chase down the breakaway group. Mackenzie was number four. She dug deep to pull the three others with her. When it was her turn to peel off, she noticed she had closed the gap on the lead group. Mackenzie held tight to Lisa's wheel.

At last, they were within the last mile to the finish. The sprint was on. Lisa took the lead for Dynamo. Mackenzie felt a rush of adrenaline. She somehow had energy to spare. Behind Lisa's wheel, Mackenzie could hear Lisa's erratic breathing. Lisa flicked her elbow signaling Mackenzie to take the lead. As Lisa dropped back, Mackenzie encouraged, "Here we go. All in." She felt Lisa pull in behind her wheel, trying to hold on. The other two Dynamo riders weren't able to keep up.

Mackenzie decided that her role was to slingshot Lisa past Team Electric. Her lungs and legs were burning, but she knew she had more. Push, pull, push, pull. *Finish it, Z. All in.* She saw the three yellow jerseys ahead. The last rider had a purple helmet with a long, dark, purple-hued braid down her back.

Mackenzie's competitive instincts kicked into overdrive when she saw Jules ahead of her. She knew she'd have to dig deeper to hook on to the team ahead of them and she was willing to lay it all on the line. She rose from her seat to gain more power. Push, pull, push, pull. Sweat dripped from her forehead and stung her eyes. She squinted. She was on Jules' wheel. This was it. *All in. Finish it.* She repeated with the push and pull rhythm.

On the next turn, Mackenzie started creeping on the left side, but the yellow jerseys started to box her out. She saw the last right curve ahead, and her instincts told her to take an unexpected line. She signaled to Lisa to take the high side; she was going to take the inside line.

Makenzie edged out then sharply attacked the line towards the inside curve. Her move surprised Jules who reacted by trying to box her in towards the gravel on the road shoulder. In doing so, Jules's pedal clipped Mackenzie's front tire, and in a split second, Mackenzie looked toward the gravel, and her bike veered dangerously toward a crash.

Knowing that a rider steers where she stares, Mackenzie quickly focused back on the road before her and re-positioned her body to keep upright. After clipping Mackenzie, Jules lost her balance and pedal rhythm. The leading yellow jersey dropped back at the same time Jules lost momentum, which confused the front rider, who didn't know where to land back in the paceline. Mackenzie's lungs were burning, and she could feel her quads tightening. The commotion created a hole for Mackenzie to sprint through, and adrenaline rushed through her as she pushed through and grabbed the wheel of the remaining yellow jersey. Lisa pulled back in behind Mackenzie as they heard the announcer at the finish line. Lisa, almost inaudibly, croaked ahead to Mackenzie, "Split right."

Lisa had practiced this with the team at their last ride, and this was the moment to apply their practice on the racecourse. Split seconds later, Lisa slingshot off Mackenzie's wheel and split to the left side of the yellow jersey. Mackenzie slingshot off the yellow jersey's wheel and split right. The blur of blue jerseys left the yellow jersey in their dust as they crossed the finish line, side by side.

Mackenzie wheeled her bike off to the side and crumpled to the ground. Lisa was by her side moments later, clearly in better shape than Mackenzie. "Z! That was a risky move, taking that line. I thought you were a goner," Lisa shook her head at Mackenzie. "I owe you one. You're an animal! I can't believe we won!"

Mackenzie, weak and feeling nauseous, managed to raise her hand to give Lisa a high five. Then she turned her head away and puked on the sidewalk.

"Woah. Someone went over her lactate threshold. Let's get you walking around with some electrolytes," Lisa coached.

"Not yet," Mackenzie squeaked. "I think I need to sit here for a moment."

Mackenzie looked up, and across the road, she saw a yellow jersey hunched over with a purple-hued braid hanging to her side. Wes was next to Jules, his face concerned. Suddenly, Jules swatted him away and yelled something unintelligible. Wes shook his head, shrugged his shoulders, and backed away slowly.

"Well, at least you're doing better than Jules right now," Lisa commented.

Mackenzie suddenly felt sorry for her competitor who was now hunched over and alone, "Poor Jules."

"Poor Jules? You're not thinking clearly. Jules chose her path. If we can learn anything from Jules, it's that Jules deposited all of her jewels in the wrong bank account and is now paying the price for her skewed priorities."

Mackenzie appreciated Lisa's analogy, "You win. Good call."

"Or a collar of jewels can choke you. Don't bike with Jules," Lisa chuckled.

"How can you be this peppy after that race?" Mackenzie wondered aloud.

"I've been training harder than you for a greater amount of time. You put everything into that race, but this is likely the first time you've pushed yourself beyond your threshold. I put everything out there in the race, but I've been training beyond my threshold, doing intervals, for a few years. With years of my intense interval training, my body has been conditioned to recover quicker than yours. You have to go slow to go fast."

Mackenzie, stunned, stared at Lisa and asked, "Did JD teach you that?"

A sly smile spread across Lisa's face. Mackenzie knew to listen closely. She knew that Lisa was going to tell her something important. "Z, I used to ride solo. There is no draft riding solo. JD taught me that life is better in the paceline."

Lisa put her arm under Mackenzie's elbow to lift her up. "Let's go join the team. I think they're going to be excited to celebrate with you."

DEVELOPING TRUST
Chapter 54

Despite her low-key Sunday spent recovering from Saturday's race, 6 AM on Monday morning rolled around way too quickly. Mackenzie's whole body hurt. Lisa had tried to give her advice on recovery fluids and food as Lisa drove her home, but Mackenzie couldn't remember anything. *Apparently, one needs oxygen for her brain to function*; she vaguely remembered telling herself.

Mackenzie arrived at the yoga studio and looked around for Karen amidst the groups mingling in yoga spandex. Karen was engaged in conversation with a tall, muscular woman with blue mirrored sunglasses on her head.

Although Mackenzie's water bottle was full, she decided that grabbing a drink from the water fountain would allow her to casually wave at Karen as she walked by. As she lifted her hand to wave, the woman talking to Karen turned her head and shouted, "Z?!" The woman quickly turned back to Karen, "Excuse me a moment, Karen, I've got to congratulate this champion over here."

"Brenda!" Mackenzie exclaimed at her teammate's unexpected presence in the studio.

"Z. Lisa told me how you pulled her to victory! What an incredible race! I saw you at the finish line but didn't get to talk with you. You seemed to be having an important meeting with the sidewalk."

Mackenzie shook her head, laughing at Brenda. "Hey, you told me to leave it all out there!"

Brenda gave her a strong side hug. Mackenzie managed to look towards Karen, "Good morning, Karen."

"Karen, do you know this hero?" Brenda squeezed Mackenzie again and looked at Karen. "This woman had the most determination I've ever heard about on a race course. She just started cycling with our team a month ago. She got clipped in the race, somehow stayed upright, and pulled our captain and team to victory! In her first cycling race ever!" She turned to Mackenzie, "That really was something. Your effort made a huge impression on the whole team. I'm glad I'm on your team, Z."

Karen just stood there, taking it all in, with an interested look on her face.

"Thanks, Bren. There's no way we would have been in any position to win without the Dynamo paceline," Mackenzie acknowledged. "We did good together, huh?"

"We sure did, Z. We sure did. You here to stretch out your sore muscles?" Brenda asked.

Mackenzie motioned to Karen and said, "I'm actually here meeting Karen this morning. How do you two know each other?"

"Really? Aren't you full of surprises, Z? Well, Karen and I go way back. We were both on the board of the Boys and Girls Club in Des Moines. She whipped our board into shape, didn't you, Kare?"

"Well, someone had to bring order to the chaos," Karen responded then turned her head to Mackenzie added, "Let's get settled, shall we?"

Although Mackenzie wanted to continue this small talk,

Karen was clearly all business and efficiency, including with her yoga practice. Mackenzie took her cue and purchased their passes. As they walked over the threshold of the studio, they instinctively obeyed the unwritten code of silence during the yoga session.

Mackenzie's whole body was still sore from the race. A far cry from any label of a yogi, she just did her best to not tip over during the cow pose. She had already perfected the cow tipping move and didn't intend to showcase that again.

During the last ten minutes of the session, Mackenzie started thinking about her upcoming coffee conversation with Karen. The yoga instructor whispered, "In these last few minutes, I want you to choose a word to focus on; a word that brings your mind to a higher level. Meditate on that word. Say that word over and over again. Be mindful of that word. Let that word take you to a new level of consciousness…"

Mackenzie considered the instructor's guidance. The word 'listen' popped into her mind. "Listen. Listen. Listen," she repeated to herself.

The yoga studio was conveniently located next to a hip coffee shop. Karen and Mackenzie waved good-bye to Brenda and walked next door for a cup of caffeine. Mackenzie took note of Karen's order and paid for their drinks. Mackenzie steered them toward a table in the back and said, "Karen, thank you for saying 'yes' to yoga! I really needed that. How did that go for you?"

"That was nice; I needed that as well. Life and work get so busy that I find it hard to slow down sometimes."

"I agree. Sometimes I just need someone to stop me and tell me to breathe!" Mackenzie admitted.

Karen nodded in agreement and asked, "Which word did you focus on in those last few minutes?"

Mackenzie tensed. Telling Karen her word felt too vulnerable. But, maybe that's where she needed to start. "The word was

'Listen.' So I do hope to be able to listen to you this morning. What was your word, Karen?"

Karen nodded and pursed her lips. "Mackenzie, I think I misjudged you at my office. After my frustration with our young workers recently quitting without notice, I looked down upon anyone around your age. I can tell from what Brenda said this morning and from what I see with your follow-up that you're a hard worker and are willing to put in the time to make things work. I like that."

Mackenzie noticed that Karen did not answer her question, but felt it wasn't the right time to bring it up again. So, instead, she responded, "Thank you, Karen. That means a lot coming from you. I've heard that you are a woman who gets things done and gets them done right the first time. It sounds like you did the same with the Boys and Girls Club board. I'd love to hear why you chose to spend your time with that organization."

For the next fifteen minutes, Mackenzie uncovered more of Karen's personality, and a peek into her pain. She and her husband couldn't have children of their own, so they poured into the lives of the Boys and Girls Club's at-risk children. Karen was concerned about big issues like reducing crime, boosting school standards, and improving public morality. She was confident in her ability to get the Club's finances back on track and to implement a system to organize duties and responsibilities would serve the at-risk kids in the upcoming generations.

Mackenzie praised her, "You are clearly a person who gives generously of her time and energy." She then summarized, "So, Karen, what I ultimately hear you say is that you value highly organized systems where individuals within organizations can efficiently maximize their focus on what they do best. I think it's safe to assume that you do the same in your work at Whitman. Would you agree?"

Karen leaned in, "I have to tell you something, Mackenzie. After you left my office at our first meeting, Ted Whitman stopped by my office to ask me how our meeting went. I was busy, and I curtly told him, 'I don't see us using their technology.' He looked at me and shook his head. He said, 'Karen, I don't have a clue whether we want to buy their technology or not. What I do know is that young woman is the type of employee that I want you to hire.'

"I didn't know how to respond. I realized I was looking at you with the wrong perspective. Ted saw something in you that I didn't have the patience to see. Brenda and your cycling team have seen your perseverance and drive that I didn't take time to notice. Mackenzie, I'd like to continue this conversation and would like you to think about a career with Whitman Distributing. We need people like you to bring a new energy into our company."

Makenzie was astonished. *What would JD do in this situation? You can't get what you want until they get what they want. Go slow to go fast. Make deposits. Favorable access to get a meeting. Which one is it?* The silence remained.

Karen, looking relaxed for the first time, said, "This has been a delightful way to start off the week. How about we schedule next Monday for another round of yoga and coffee?"

Mackenzie, relieved that Karen set up their next meeting, regained her composure and asked, "If there were a way for you to show me around Whitman so I could learn more about your company, would that be of interest to you?"

"Definitely. When we walk around, I would also like to hear your thoughts about how more efficient and effective training would result in higher retention of Whitman employees. And I'll tell you about a few positions at Whitman where I think you could really make an impact."

Mackenzie responded, "Thank you, Karen. I always aim to make a positive impact. Let's find out if it would be best for the company to do that as a consultant for Whitman or as an employee."

Karen returned Mackenzie's smile and said, "That sounds like a great idea."

As they stood up to leave, Mackenzie stated, "I'm still curious, though. What was the word you focused on at the end of yoga?"

"It was not exactly a deep word. It was 'coffee.'" Karen let out a loud noise, like a cackle that hadn't been heard very often. Mackenzie, once she recognized it as a laugh, joined in.

CLIPPED

Chapter 55

When Mackenzie arrived at work that morning, she tackled two important calls she needed to make. Her first call was to Mr. Garcia to update him on her progress with Whitman Distributing. He surprised her by answering her call.

"Mr. Garcia, thank you for taking my call. Karen and I made excellent progress this morning, and she has invited me back to Whitman Distributing to discuss their current training and hiring processes."

"Great work, Mackenzie. With your win last week you're continuing to gain momentum."

Mackenzie answered, "I have you to thank for re-opening the door with Karen. Your willingness to extend your favorable access to me resulted in a positive opportunity for the entire company."

"Well, you're welcome!" Mr. Garcia exclaimed. "I started to reflect on my lawn mowing days and recognized that when one neighbor recommended me to the next, I started gaining momentum. It wasn't just my hard work in knocking on hundreds of doors. My persistence was noticed, but it took someone's trust in me to help me take my ambition to the next level. Now that I know you're willing and able to follow-up for our company, let me know if I can make any more phone calls for you, similar to the one that opened up the door to Karen."

Mackenzie was surprised by his generous offer of creating a draft for her and quickly responded, "Thank you, Mr. Garcia. If there were a way for me to vet five strong suspects with connections to you and get them to you later today, then would you be willing to call each of them by next Wednesday?"

"Way to be on it, Mackenzie. Yes, I'll do that for you. And how are you doing with the content creation from JD and Bill?" Mr. Garcia inquired.

"That is in process. When is the next time you'll be in Des Moines, Mr. Garcia?"

"I don't have anything on the calendar yet. What do you have in mind?" he responded.

"I'd like to set up a lunch with you, Stan, JD, Bill, and myself. JD and Bill mentioned they'd like to catch up with you," Mackenzie offered.

"You name the date, and I'll get the travel booked. Good work, Mackenzie. Send me those suspects and let's make it happen."

"Will do, Mr. Garcia. Thank you."

Mackenzie hung up the phone and knew to make her next important phone call. The call was transferred to Bill, and although he sounded tired, he told her to meet him at Reichardt's store. She grabbed the company car keys and made her way to the elevator.

She passed by Tommy's desk and stopped. She had learned a few things since she felt sucker-punched by Tommy taking over her lead with Dr. Evan. "Hey, Tommy. Have you made any progress with Dr. Evan?"

Tommy furrowed his brow, wary of her question, "Some. Still working on it. Why?"

Mackenzie knew how to start building a paceline at work and answered, "I found out that his son wants to be a football kicker when he gets older. It crossed my mind that he might want some coaching…"

Tommy raised his eyebrows, "Really? That's a great idea!" He paused and added, "Ya know, I felt kinda bad that I took Dr. Evan as a prospect after you introduced me to him. Are you mad about that?"

Mackenzie admitted, "I was. At first. Then I realized that no one really owns a prospect until she or he makes the sale. It's all fair game until that point, and we will all do better as a company if we start working as a team. I hope Dr. Evan opens a few doors for you. The better you succeed, the better we all succeed."

Mackenzie walked away feeling good about making another deposit into Tommy. The day before, she had stumbled across an African proverb that read, "If you want to go fast, go alone. If you want to go far, go together." That rang true with JD's notion of the paceline, and the truth of it was beginning to make a lot of sense. After she pressed the elevator's down button, she sensed someone behind her. She turned to see Stan with a scowl on his face. Mackenzie was on a roll with making deposits and decided Stan probably needed some encouragement too, "Hey, Stan. How are you doing?"

"How am I doing? I think a better question is, 'How are you doing?'" Stan barked.

Mackenzie was taken by surprise with his bitter tone but remained upbeat, "We have our first sale on the board, and we're going to get a few more in the paceline."

"And who are you using to get those?" Stan shot back.

Mackenzie was stunned by his stab, "What are you talking about?"

Stan glared at her, "Mackenzie, I'm warning you. I will get HR involved. I just listened to a voicemail from Tony. No other new salesperson has the ear of the CEO. I suggest that you stop using your female wiles to get preferential treatment. I don't know what game you're playing, but I strongly suggest that you back off and use your own networks to move forward from now on."

"What?!" Mackenzie's breath was knocked clear out of her. She felt anger welling up deep inside her, "I can't believe you just said that. You are so, so...so wrong about me."

Mackenzie was at a loss for words and quickly turned and walked straight to the stairs, her indignation rising with every step. By the time she hit the last stair, furious, hot tears had stained her face. She didn't even know what to do next. She squeezed the keys in her hand, sprinted to the car, and locked the doors once she was inside.

She wanted to get as far away from the office as possible. She sped out of the parking lot, wheels squealing as she made her first turn, and drove straight towards Reichardt's Clothing Store. Taking a spot in the back parking lot, she rested her head on the steering wheel and sobbed.

After ten minutes of replaying the scene with Stan in her head over and over again, and getting more offended and outraged every time because of his unjust accusations, she looked at herself in the rear view mirror and remembered the last time her eyes looked this bleary. The failed first in-person meeting with Karen Smith at Whitman had seemed like her worst professional moment, but it now seemed insignificant. She decided to pull herself together and go inside to ask for advice from the man who had been kicked in the teeth.

LEADING A LIFE OF SIGNIFICANCE
Chapter 56

Mackenzie waved to Henry as she walked in the door and made her way back to Bill's open office door. She sat down in the chair across from his desk and saw Bill in a wheelchair with his broken leg sticking out straight. She said, "Bill, I need to know that you're okay. Are you okay?"

"It looks like I'm more okay than you are! What happened to you? You look like you've been in a fight with a Canadian football team."

"Yeah, had a rough conversation before I drove over here. But, really, it's nothing. What did your doctors say?" Mackenzie was still too fragile to bring up Stan's accusations. She needed to focus on someone else.

"The docs had bad news and good news. The bad news is that I have cancer. Yeah, not what I wanted to hear. The good news is that it hasn't spread like they originally thought. It's localized, and they can remove it with a few surgeries."

"Woah. When are your surgeries?" Mackenzie asked, trying not to express her shock from his news.

"Scheduled for late next week. It will be fine. I have a great team of doctors. And now, back to you, what are you dealing with?"

Mackenzie felt shallow bringing up her needs when Bill was dealing with cancer. She tried to downplay it. "It's nothing. Definitely nothing in comparison, Bill. It's just that my manager accused me of using my 'female wiles' to get ahead." She emphasized the female wiles with air quotes and shook her head, unable to shake her distress despite her attempt.

"From what I know of you, that doesn't sound anything like you. You haven't even hit on me once!" Bill's laugh boomed off the walls.

Mackenzie cracked a smile at her friend in his late eighties, "Haha, Bill. Very funny."

She paused, but Bill didn't fill the void, so she continued, "I just started gaining momentum, and I feel like he attacked me, attacked my character. Am I over-reacting?"

Bill considered what he wanted to say, and then said, "Mackenzie, in sales and in life, you will have set-backs. Some will be professional, some will be personal, and some will be both. People you thought you could trust will get jealous of you and purposely take you down. Most people aren't trying to hurt you or take advantage of you; they are just trying to keep themselves above the waterline, and sometimes they'll force you underwater in order to feel like they can breathe.

"Most of us, at many points in our lives, lead lives of quiet desperation. When people try to take you down, remember that you don't know what it is they are dealing with in their life. Their anger may have nothing to do with you; it's likely something in their own lives that they are fighting against.

"When you're in the thick of a distressing event, it's a big deal. It feels all-consuming. But, when you live as long as I have, you have time to reflect on those traumatic experiences and realize that they can shape you into something stronger. With post-traumatic growth, you have the opportunity to refine your character. And you usually can't be alone to have the post-traumatic growth because you often can't see past yourself to understand the bigger picture."

Mackenzie nodded.

"In order to let others in, you have to reach out and ask someone who's not in the traumatic trenches with you. You need someone who has a different perspective, and you need to be willing to say 'Okay, I'm ready to listen to someone other than myself.'

"When you've got a broken leg, or have cancer, or someone falsely accuses you, you'll want some friends who can walk alongside to encourage you and some other friends who can light a fire under your ass and tell you not to quit. Those are the people who you've made deposits into, day after day, year after year. And you've allowed them to do the same for you. Some moments you're the one pulling them, other moments, they are pulling you. These people make up your personal paceline."

Mackenzie nodded. JD and Bill had been purposeful in creating a paceline for her. She started thinking about how lucky she was that JD had chosen to invest in and challenge her. *Luck. It is not luck!* She reminded herself. *But, it's also more than just positioning and utilizing the Steps and the Rules.* She knew in her soul that she still didn't understand the bigger picture with everything and everyone working together for her and she also knew that she had a responsibility to pay this favor forward.

Bill began again, "JD's favorable access lessons are not just about teaching how you can win more sales or material things in the end. JD's favorable access lessons are about building relationships and taking the long-range view. By getting your focus off of yourself, you focus on the people around you, figuring out how to give to them, not just at what you want to gain from them. In doing this, you'll lead a life of significance to others which, in turn, brings you fulfillment."

Mackenzie agreed but didn't know what else to add. So she just nodded again and let Bill continue.

"So this manager of yours may be living a life of quiet desperation. He sees you gaining momentum and growing in confidence. I'm not making an excuse for him, just stating a different perspective. What he said was totally misguided, and it likely won't be the last time you'll hear a comment like that. So, take a step back and think about your options. Let's start where you are right now. What your options?"

"I can call HR and file a complaint, I can do nothing and try to ignore it, or I can quit," Mackenzie uttered.

"Yep, those are options. If there were a way for you to use your favorable access and draw the line with this guy, would you be interested in that?" Bill questioned.

"What do you mean by that?" Mackenzie asked.

Bill answered, "In my lifetime, I've also used my power many times to intimidate people. In later years, I had people stand up to me and yell back at me, or quit, and others who have taken a more mature path. It took a few people taking the more mature path to help me recognize that everyone does not have the same privilege as me, a man in a position of power. It is vital, especially in your position as a young woman without the power, that you know how to stand up for yourself in a way that stops the harassing behavior and allows you to continue on your path ahead."

Mackenzie confirmed, "That's exactly what I want and need right now. So what can I do?"

Bill answered, "Your manager accused you of having an unprofessional relationship in order to get ahead. Likely this is due to the CEO spending more energy on you than on him. You have to know that you do not deserve this treatment, that you are strong enough to stand up to it, and that you can both learn and grow from these situations. I don't know what this guy is dealing with in his life, but he is trying to intimidate you with his power. In order for you to come out better on the other side, you need to address the situation with maturity, and you need back-up."

"Back-up?" Mackenzie inquired.

"If there were a way for you to let your manager know that he was out of line, that his comments will not be tolerated again, and make your working relationship better with your manager moving forward, would you be interested in how to do that?"

"Of course," Mackenzie, even knowing about alignment questions, couldn't help but agree that she did want all three outcomes.

Bill began again, "If there were a way for you to go back to work, bring him up to speed on what you are doing, tell him you would like to introduce him to me, and set up a meeting with both of you meeting me here in my office, would you be willing to do that?"

Mackenzie started to feel more optimistic about her situation with Bill on her side, "Definitely."

"Great. Because your manager is Stan Silinger, correct?" Bill asked.

How does Bill know Stan? Mackenzie thought.

Bill answered Mackenzie's unasked question, "Stan has been trying to meet with me for years, but I didn't like his approach. So, by you setting up this meeting with me for him, you are making a deposit. Then, you gently shift gears. You calmly tell him that what he assumed of you was inappropriate and unprofessional. You tell him that you don't know what is going on in his life right now to cause him to say something like that and you will forgive him of this one-time inappropriate behavior. You expect him never to cross that line again. Then, in our meeting, we'll talk next steps on the content piece for clothing stores, and I'll get to praise your hard work and how you've applied what you've learned. I most certainly will not mention the situation, but he will see, first-hand, how you handle yourself with integrity."

"Okay, Bill," Mackenzie nodded. "Thank you. It means a lot to me that you have my back on this. But with your surgeries next week, when can we meet?"

"Sooner rather than later. How about early next week?"

"I'll go back and set that up right now," Mackenzie said.

"Let me know how it goes. Some men make bad choices and continue to do so. Some men learn from their mistakes and become better. Some take longer than others to realize the err of their ways. It took me longer than most to figure out that I needed to do better. When you can work through a tough situation and come to an understanding, you'll both be stronger for it."

"I hear you. Thank you, again, Bill," Mackenzie stated earnestly, grateful that he continued to walk alongside her and help her through this situation. She and Bill continued talking and before she left his office, he handed her a book to read.

CHANGING COURSE
Chapter 57

Mackenzie sat down at the bar to order a beer. She was early for her meet-up with Luke but knew she needed to unwind from work before they met. The meeting with Stan went better than she expected. He was surprised by her offer to set up a meeting with Bill Reichardt. Stan looked relieved as if he expected that she wouldn't mention his earlier accusation. She was glad that she took the high road.

Starting with a goodwill gesture had allowed both of them to relax and address the underlying issue with calm emotions. Although Stan did not apologize, he did nod his head in agreement when she corrected their misunderstanding. She attempted to set clear boundaries which at least gave her the impression that he would not cross that line again.

She looked up to get the bartender's attention. Before she had a chance to order a beer, a friendly voice shouted, "Mackenzie!"

Mackenzie turned around to see her former college track teammate walking towards her. Mackenzie had long admired this former teammate; she was a fierce competitor, always said exactly what was on her mind, and didn't accept any excuses for not training hard. "It's been too long! So good to see you."

"You too! You drinking alone?" she asked.

"Ha. It does look that way, huh?" Mackenzie smiled, "No, I'm just early for meeting a friend for drinks. You want to join us?"

"That depends. Who are you meeting?" True to her character, without a filter, her former teammate always charged straight to the point.

"His name is Luke. Actually, you might know him from college. Do you remember the guy who dated our long-jumper with the pink hair?"

"Yes, I totally remember him! I saw him out at a party last weekend, come to think of it. He must have started working out. I don't remember him being that buff. You two dating?"

"No, we are not dating," Mackenzie responded quickly.

"You should date him," her teammate interjected.

"What? No, we're just friends. He's not my type, anyway," Mackenzie added.

"Not your type?" She questioned, eyebrows raised.

"Miss Long-Jumper told me all about his dark and gloomy side, so it's best to stay friends," Mackenzie answered confidently.

"Consider the source, my friend. And consider yourself too. It's not like you were Miss Sunshine after you busted your knee. We all go through dark seasons in our lives. But hey, if good-looking, smart, and successful isn't your type, then put in a good word for me, okay?" She slugged her on the shoulder. "I'm late meeting with some friends in the back, but let's get together soon, alright?"

"Sounds like a plan. See you soon." Mackenzie shook her head as she watched her friend walk to the back of the restaurant. She marveled at how candid her teammate continued to be, and her comments made her question why she didn't want more than friendship with Luke.

She has a point, Mackenzie conceded. *My pink-haired long-jump friend was a drama queen. Luke may not have been the most considerate person in college, but yeah, we all go through some dark seasons at some point in our lives. And he is sneaky good-looking, smart, and has shown himself to be rather thoughtful lately. But, I don't think he's into me. Or maybe it's me? Maybe I'm not ready for a relationship. I probably have some sort of deep-seated Daddy-issues; afraid to commit because I know it won't last. Yeah, that sounds about right.*

As Mackenzie continued to psychoanalyze herself, a restaurant host approached her, tapped her on the shoulder and asked, "A wild guess here. Are you Mackenzie?"

"Yes, how did you know?" She answered, thinking that Luke might be pulling another no-show.

"A guy named Luke called and said there might be a smoking hot brunette here with emerald green eyes who loves Exile beer." The host winked and added, "You must be that someone. He wanted to make sure you were properly welcomed and seated at a special table."

Mackenzie gave the host a puzzled look and followed him to a table set in the corner, with a frosted glass of Exile beer beside the centerpiece, an orchid with half of its buds in bloom, displaying a white and purple pattern on the petals. She returned her attention back to the host when he started talking again, "Your guy said he'd be here in a few minutes. He told me that Exile's Pilsner is your favorite. If not, I'll go back and get you whatever you'd like."

"No. No, this is great. I'm just surprised is all," she said as she sat down at the table, thinking, *is this a date? Wait, I asked him out, didn't I?*

She leaned back in her chair and took a gulp of her beer. She looked at the eccentric craft beer bottle that the host had set across from her for Luke. The unique craft label and the orchid next to it, showing off its purple patterns, made her think about what she was wearing. She knew that she looked nice in her work attire, but perhaps this would have been a good opportunity to have fun with her clothes, as Bill had suggested when it was an appropriate setting. She thought, *well, at least I'm not wearing wrinkled khakis! No matter what I'm wearing, being ushered to a private table with my favorite beer waiting for me after this emotional roller-coaster day I survived is undoubtedly a nice break.*

Luke walked in a few minutes later and smiled at her from across the room. Her stomach flipped as she noticed that he looked rather handsome in his jeans, jacket, and button-down, which was a departure from his normal casual look. He seemed confident, yet she detected a subtle air of uncertainty about him. Mackenzie stood up, not knowing how to greet him. *Hug? Fist bump? Side-hug and handshake?*

Luke answered her question with a full embrace, "It's really good to see you, Mackenzie. You arrived earlier than I expected."

"Yeah, I walked over straight from work and thought I'd buy a beer before you got here. You beat me to it," she awkwardly stammered. She was suddenly nervous and didn't know what to say next.

"Well, cheers, Mackenzie," he smiled sweetly and clinked her glass with his. "Let's toast to you. Your bike race was unbelievable!"

Mackenzie blushed. She hadn't seen Luke after the race because once she and Lisa shuffled over to the Dynamo team, the team swarmed her and then Lisa promptly drove her home to recover. Mackenzie was thankful for a non-emotional topic to discuss and relaxed. "Thanks for coming out to see the race, Luke. That really meant a lot. Sorry I didn't see you afterwards. My recovery wasn't pretty."

Luke laughed, "You really went beyond your threshold. You

raced tough. I happened to be watching at the point in the race when you made your move from fourth to second. That move took a lot of moxie. How did you know to take that line on the inside?"

"I'm not totally sure. Something inside me clicked when I saw a different line. My team set me up to be in the top group because Lisa believed I could hang in there. We had all spent time pulling for each other in practice and in the race. I wanted to win. But this time it wasn't just for myself; I wanted to win for my team."

She knew there would have been no way to achieve on her own what was only possible through her paceline's full commitment to each other and the process. Ironically, that's how she knew it would feel at OnBoardMobile if the sales team started pulling for each other in a similar fashion if only Stan could get on board. The way JD's Steps & Rules were captured and explained using a paceline made so much sense to her now, especially after racing for Dynamo. *But, this is no time to think about the Steps & Rules,* she thought to herself, *I might be on a date right now! The Steps & Rules don't apply to dating.*

Luke's expression turned serious, "I know these past few years have been really difficult for you. In the last few weeks, I've seen you take charge of your life again, and I think you're getting back to being the Mackenzie that you are meant to be."

Mackenzie, surprised by his insight, responded, "Thanks for noticing, Luke. I have been working really hard in so many areas of my life. And, I have you to thank for indirectly pushing me into position to meet JD and Bill. They've helped me to see that the physical, mental, emotional, and spiritual aspects of my life are all connected."

Luke interjected, "Can you help me with that?"

Without hesitation, Mackenzie responded, "I've just begun learning about this, but I think we could help each other figure more of this out. Mr. Reichardt shared a gift with me that I think I'm supposed to share with others. After his recent hospital stay, he said, 'I've never been afraid of dying…but I've always been afraid of not living. I don't want just to live; I want to be fully alive.' He explained the connections between the physical, mental, emotional, and spiritual parts of living fully engaged in all of these areas. Then he gave me a book that talked about all of the connections." She paused to gauge Luke's interest. He was all in.

Mackenzie continued, "So as I began to get in better shape with cycling, I started to see an improvement in my mental state and emotional attitude. When I reflect on all that's happened in the last month, I know there's more than just coincidence at work; there is a greater power pulling all of these lessons together. I don't understand the spiritual side of all this, but I think it's somehow the key that brings it all together."

Despite her original thinking that a date is no place for the Steps & Rules, she recalled JD's Rule 3: 'Questions are rarely questions. Find the why.' She probed, "But, tell me why you'd like to hear about this."

Luke ventured, "You've got this renewed energy about you, and it makes me want to hang around you even more."

Mackenzie stopped breathing. She immediately understood that this was a crucial moment. She recognized it as an alignment opportunity.

When Luke arrived at Exile, she knew that she wanted to spend more time with him. He was worth taking a risk on, worth facing her fear of abandonment. This was the moment where she could continue protecting herself or have the courage to pursue something that deep down, she knew she desired. She turned her head to the side slightly, and playfully inquired, "If there were a way that we could hang out more often would you be up for that?"

Luke's smile spread across his face. Without saying a word, he stood up and walked two steps around the small table between them. Mackenzie didn't move. Luke took her hand and pulled her up towards him. She willingly stepped in.

He looked into her eyes and asked, "What are the things you need from me in order to make this happen?"

She returned his gaze and aligned her lips with his.

THE BEST SELLER
Chapter 58

JD and Bill sat at a comfortable table in the back of the Dynamo Coffee Shop. The first things Mackenzie saw when she walked in were the giant bandages on both sides of Bill's neck. She had dropped off a six-pack of Coors Light at his store earlier with a note saying she was rooting for him to get the cancer cleared from his body and make a full recovery. Looking at Bill's neck now, though, along with his broken leg and additional bandages, she realized that a six-pack was woefully insufficient. He needed a keg.

"Good morning, Bill and JD. Bill, it's really good to see how well you're recovering from your surgery!" Mackenzie beamed, knowing that he likely felt worse than he looked.

"Mackenzie, that's kind of you. I feel like I've been hit by the entire Canadian football team again. But I'll tell you what I've learned. Now that I have these giant bandages on my neck and this cast on my leg, my desperation isn't so silent. 'For whatever is hidden is meant to be disclosed, and whatever is concealed is meant to be brought out in the open.'

"There's absolutely no hiding these wounds unless I locked myself in my house, and there's no way in hell I'm staying cooped up inside. I'd go crazy. Besides, there's no good reason to remain in the dark and cover up my weaknesses. As I've hobbled around, people everywhere have never been this helpful to me! I should have bandaged myself up a long time ago! Hawhawhaw!"

Mackenzie and JD laughed with him. Bill sat back and continued, "It just goes to show you, that when we reveal our wounds or struggles in a position of humility, most people respond to our needs with genuine kindness or outright terror. Either way, we quickly figure out where we stand."

JD nodded, allowing a small silence before adding, "I agree. At the root of it all, we want to be understood. Our needs, wants, desires, pain...no matter if it's in our personal or professional lives. We all need someone to listen and ask us questions to reveal what is underneath. Most people won't simply reveal their wounds to us, and most will not have the obvious bandages and casts to lead us to the source of their pain. That's why embracing and implementing the Steps & Rules with intentionality are so important."

Mackenzie nodded and took that as her cue to be intentional with what she had learned from these two men. She pulled out two papers from her satchel, slid them across the table and started, "I wrote out an agenda for this morning. Is there anything on here that either one of you would like to start with specifically or add to this agenda?"

JD smiled, "Mackenzie, excellent practice. You are setting yourself up for success. Let's start right where you are with what you've got. I'm glad we've been able to ride alongside you thus far in your journey. Let's make this ride count."

Mackenzie acknowledged, "JD and Bill, I cannot thank you enough for agreeing to capture your life's lessons in a format for others to learn from. I'm only just beginning to understand why and how the sales process works. You've taught me how important it is to invest in and prioritize relationships. I'm realizing that favorable access and demand-pull are the natural outcomes of the deposits that we make in people's lives and the value we bring. When we are motivated to differentiate our efforts and truly develop relationships, then quality and authenticity are the results." Mackenzie grinned and added, "And there just isn't any substitute for…"

"Quality," JD chimed in.

Bill started laughing and couldn't resist, "And I'll see to it. Because I'm here. I'm Bill Reichardt, and I own the store."

Mackenzie's gratefulness overflowed. In a short period of time, JD and Bill had opened her eyes to see the world of business and relationships through a lens of quality. They had reminded her that she could confidently own her direction in life when she invested her value into others and worked with others, not against them. In the competitive world of sales, working for and with others seemed counterintuitive, but once she began to see the outcomes of those investments, it made sense.

JD interjected, "Before we get started, I did want to ask you about your race last Saturday. I heard you pulled quite a move at the race and ended up winning the whole dang thing. What happened to 'go slow to go fast'?" JD chuckled.

"Sometimes you just have to go with your instinct," she smirked, recalling JD's line.

"Right on, Mackenzie. Just like you did in the race, often you have to take a different line, you have to take a risk and go all in," JD declared.

Mackenzie leaned back in her chair, mulling over what JD said. The thought struck her, "JD, I didn't think about it like that when I was in the race. As I said, I was just going with my gut. But I think you're right on point. I knew in my mind that I'd have to take a risk, to take a different line, in order to shake things up. Just like at work. By learning about your Steps &

Rules, practicing and applying them to my sales techniques, it's helped shake me out of the rut I was in."

Mackenzie continued, "Trying out your demand-pull tactics were risky and did have consequences where I almost crashed. When I applied the Steps & Rules, my manager misunderstood what I was doing and wanted to fire me because of it. But, it's made all the difference for me. It's shown me that the sales process is more than numbers and metrics; it's about adding value, solving problems, and building relationships. This is reminding me that we can't just read or hear about certain strategies, we have to put them into practice in a race, in real life when the pressure is on. Which makes me think again about these Steps & Rules. How will we get others to not just study the demand-pull strategies, but to put all of the Steps & Rules into practice?"

JD nodded, "Great question. I'd like to hear your answer to that."

"I'm thinking you might have a better perspective, JD," Mackenzie smiled.

JD laughed, "It will be up to you and how you want to teach through the Steps & Rules, Mackenzie. But one thing I do know is that you practice cycling both individually and as a team in a paceline. Sales follow the same structure."

Mackenzie lit up, "JD, Bill, if there were a way to create a team atmosphere, like some sort of Paceline Community, would you be willing to moderate a few sessions?"

JD responded, "I think we could do that."

Mackenzie, "Great! What are the things you need from me in order to make this happen?"

Bill shifted uncomfortably in his wheelchair, "A few cases of Coors Light. And a minivan with a driver who can wheel me around; preferably someone who can laugh at my jokes."

Mackenzie nodded and remarked, "Let me get this right. You need a few cases and a joyful minivan driver. Is there anything else that's stopping us from putting this Paceline Community together?"

JD looked at Bill then back at Mackenzie. He smiled and stated, "I believe that someone is on her way to becoming The Best Seller."

8 "STEPS" OF THE SALES PROCESS

Step 1: Understand your general access.
Step 2: Develop a plan to gain favorable access.
Step 3: Leverage favorable access to get a meeting.
Step 4: Set the agenda and then put the customer in control.
Step 5: Build trust through dialogue.
Step 6: Create alignment. Identify the problem and align what they need with what you can do for them.
Step 7: Control the question and the direction.
Step 8: Summarize and guide with next steps.

8 "RULES" OF THE PACELINE

Rule 1: You can't get what you want until they get what they want.
Rule 2: Go slow to go fast.
Rule 3: Questions are rarely questions. Understand the why.
Rule 4: Make significant deposits before withdrawing or asking for a loan.
Rule 5: Practice until the process becomes instinctive.
Rule 6: Communicate the value of your vision in their terms.
Rule 7: Provide perspective not just content.
Rule 8: People don't care how much you know until they know how much you care.

ACKNOWLEDGMENTS

The paceline that pulled this book together is extensive, and we are grateful for each person who rode in front, alongside us, and rotated through on this journey.

Thank you to the following paceline power players:

It was not a coincidence that Jen Sees and Katie Bishop crossed paths. They were running in opposite directions one early morning but after a quick exchange between strangers, they decided to run together and became fast friends. Jen not only stepped into the role of encourager, but also stepped into the role of editor, timeline coach, and painted the finish line for Katie and Doug.

The extended Reichardt family provided inspiration, newspaper articles, photos, audio, and VHS tapes. Austin Reichardt interviewed Bill in 1994; the resulting audiotape is a true gem. Jessica Jensen's clear memories with Bill shaped the words to describe him. Debbie Reichardt's insight of Bill and Doug provided clarity. Jim Bishop's technical ability brought all of the printed and visual documentation together.

Doug had many mentors throughout his career. Diana Diebler applied her keen mind to sales situations and shared these insights with Doug. Frank Roby's emotional intelligence taught Doug to look at situations from someone else's perspective. Both Diana and Frank influenced many of the Steps & Rules throughout Doug's career. We are forever indebted to their initial work in the Steps & Rules.

OnBoardMobile is a fictional company based on an existing company named "Inside Out LMS." You can find out more about Inside Out LMS at: https://insideoutlms.com/paceline/

Paceline groups became sounding boards, prayer warriors, and early reviewers. RSM (Rock Solid Marriages), Brave, NWG (Neighborhood Writing Group), MOPS (Mothers of Preschoolers), and CHCC bible study provided faith, feedback, and prayers for endurance when there was still a long way to go.

Ken Luallen's depth and attention to detail convinced Katie of necessary work before crossing the finish line.

Author Aimee Cohen walked her talk of being a woman who helps other women. She shared her favorable access with Katie, introducing her to key players in the publishing industry.

A big shout out to both Amber Ambrose and Lauren McDowell at the Ambrose/McDowell Agency. Their gift with words and strategy were instrumental in our marketing efforts. We are so grateful for their patience, understanding, and flexibility on our journey together.

It took a paceline. Thank you to our paceline community who gave us the wisdom to create The Best Seller.

REFERENCES

Growing up before the internet, we didn't have the world of references at our fingertips. So, when someone said something that sounded original, we often credited that wisdom to them. Many of the quotes that Bill used in his everyday speech were something he heard, liked, and repeated. We used to think that all of his thoughts were original. Now, thanks to researchers on the internet, we know that Bill was really good at selecting great thoughts from others then putting those thoughts into action and speaking them as if they were his own.

Here is where we have a duty to give credit where credit is due. Congratulations to the late Bill Reichardt who stood on the shoulders of the wise giants before him.

CHAPTER 6 - PAIN OF CHANGE:

"There will be no change until the pain of change is less than the pain of staying the same."

Similar quote by Tony Robbins: "Change happens when the pain of staying the same is greater than the pain of change."
Awaken The Giant Within, Anthony Robbins, Simon & Schuster, November 15, 1991.

CHAPTER 8 - FIRST IMPRESSIONS:

Willam Reichardt named Chicago Tribune's Big 10 MVP
Chicago Tribune, Sports, Sunday, December 16, 1951. Also: https://en.wikipedia.org/wiki/Chicago_Tribune_Silver_Football

CHAPTER 9 - CLEAN SLATE:

"Iowa would be playing Minnesota."
No. 15 Iowa vs. No. 6 Minnesota, Memorial Stadium, Minneapolis, MN; November 10, 1956. Source: Wikipedia https://en.wikipedia.org/wiki/1956_Iowa_Hawkeyes_football_team

CHAPTER 10 - I-CAPS:

"In that game I had the team doc give me 21 shots of Novocain. Coach didn't know about it. I wanted to do it. That's how important the game was to me."
"Hawkeye Legends, Lists, & Lore," Mike Finn and Chad Leistikow, Sports Publishing LLC, October 1, 1998.

"At the end of the game, the stadium crowd rushed onto the field, wrenched both of Iowa's steel goal posts from their moorings in eight feet of concrete. Echoes of 'I-O-Wa-Wa! I-

O-Wa-Wa!' were heard throughout Iowa City, as the power plant's steam whistle blasted again and again."
University of Iowa Yearbook, 1956.

CHAPTER 14 - POSITIONING:

"Demand-pull."
There is a demand-pull theory of economics, where demand pull causes different effects in the economy. To learn more: https://en.wikipedia.org/wiki/Demand-pull_theory.

"Go slow to go fast."
This quote is of unknown origin, but Abraham Lincoln was quoted saying, "Give me six hours to chop down a tree and I will spend the first four sharpening the axe." The essence of Lincoln's quote is likely where the concept was developed.

CHAPTER 15 - BOUNCES AND DEPOSITS:

"Make significant deposits before withdrawing or asking for a loan."
Dr. Stephen R. Covey's "The 7 Habits of Highly Effective People," Free Press, 1989, discusses the importance of building interdependent relationships through maintaining a positive balance in other people's emotional bank accounts. "By proactively doing things that build trust in a relationship, one makes 'deposits.'"

CHAPTER 22 - SHIFTING PERSPECTIVE:

"We all fight silent battles in our minds."

This quote is very similar to Henry David Thoreau's quote, "The mass of men lead lives of quiet desperation." This quote is also referenced in Chapters 56 and 58.

"I was always challenging people on the field and had such a loud mouth that they called me Noise Box. Noise Box and Bill the Bull."
Audiotape interview between eight year old, Austin Reichardt, and his grandfather, Bill Reichardt, in 1994.

"Practice until the process becomes instinctive."
Ralph Waldo Emerson said, "That which we persist in doing becomes easier to do, not that the nature of the thing has changed but that our power to do has increased."

"40% energy savings in the draft."
A number of cycling articles reference the energy savings in the draft to be between 20% and 50%. One of the articles we gathered this information from:
https://cyclingtips.com/2017/10/much-benefit-really-get-drafting/

CHAPTER 23 - PREPARATION MATTERS:

Paradoxical Commandments by Kent M. Keith.

Excerpt from ANYWAY: THE PARADOXICAL COMMANDMENTS: FINDING PERSONAL MEANING IN A CRAZY WORLD by Kent M. Keith, copyright © 2001 by Kent M. Keith. Used by permission of G.P. Putnam's Sons, an imprint of Penguin Publishing Group, a division of Penguin Random House LLC. All rights reserved.

CHAPTER 24 - LOGIC AND INTUITION:

"You can't get what you want until they get what they want."
Zig Ziglar said, "You can have everything in life you want, if you just help other people get what they want."

CHAPTER 27 - LIVING WITH HUMILITY:

"Pride goes before destruction and an arrogant spirit before a fall."

"Pride goes before destruction and a haughty spirit before a fall," Proverbs 16:18, The NIV Bible. Scriptures taken from the Holy Bible, New International Version®, NIV®. Copyright © 1973, 1978, 1984, 2011 by Biblica, Inc.™ Used by permission of Zondervan. All rights reserved worldwide. www.zondervan.com The "NIV" and "New International Version" are trademarks registered in the United States Patent and Trademark Office by Biblica, Inc.™

CHAPTER 28 - COMMUNICATE EFFECTIVELY:

"People don't care how much you know until they know how much you care."
This entire quote is credited to Theodore Roosevelt.

CHAPTER 33 - MEASURING COST:

Cost = Price - Value.

There is not a formal equation equal to this, which means that either the economics experts throughout the centuries have made equations too difficult or JD is brilliant or maybe this is not an official economics equation. Spoiler: It's not an official equation. This is a quasi-equation that simplifies cost, price and value in the mind of a customer. Is this too simplified? Go to www.katiebishop.us to discuss.

Low variation = higher quality = lower cost

MedCare, January 2010, the quality variation has an impact on costs and satisfaction as evidenced by the QIDS study.
Authors: Peabody JW1, Florentino J, Shimkhada R, Solon O, Quimbo S.
The similar relationship between patient-reported satisfaction and quality improvement suggests that investments in quality will raise satisfaction, perhaps even when charges are increased.

CHAPTER 40 · BREAKAWAY:

"Success is the progressive realization of a worthy ideal."
This entire quote is credited to Earl Nightengale.

"Do what you love and the money will follow."
This entire quote is credited to Marsha Sinetar.

"Begin with nothing in mind and see where you end up."
Zig Ziglar said, "If you aim at nothing, you will hit it every time."

REFERENCES

CHAPTER 58 - BEST SELLER:

'For whatever is hidden is meant to be disclosed, and whatever is concealed is meant to be brought out in the open.'
Mark 4:22, The NIV Bible.

Scriptures taken from the Holy Bible, New International Version®, NIV®. Copyright © 1973, 1978, 1984, 2011 by Biblica, Inc.™ Used by permission of Zondervan. All rights reserved worldwide. www.zondervan.com The "NIV" and "New International Version" are trademarks registered in the United States Patent and Trademark Office by Biblica, Inc.™

Other references:

Wikipedia:
   https://en.wikipedia.org/wiki/Bill_Reichardt
   https://en.wikipedia.org/wiki/Randy_Duncan

You Tube:
   Bill Reichardt's Boys State Speech, 1992:
   https://www.youtube.com/watch?v=-FzHI8J6EZY
   https://www.youtube.com/watch?v=u46l24wBTJA

Reichardt's Commercial- 1978
   https://www.youtube.com/watch?v=VbKNNF_NXAI

Reichardt's Commercial (1996)
   https://www.youtube.com/watch?v=MWGdEvamLCo

Bill Reichardt Bids Adieu
   https://www.youtube.com/watch?v=Xy8Z9MEgw78

www.ingramcontent.com/pod-product-compliance
Lightning Source LLC
Chambersburg PA
CBHW021053080526
44587CB00010B/240